PREPARE TO MEET THY TOMB

A Play

by Norman Robbins

samuelfrench.co.uk

FOR AMATEUR PRODUCTION ENQUIRIES

UNITED KINGDOM AND WORLD
EXCLUDING NORTH AMERICA
plays@samuelfrench.co.uk
020 7255 4302/01

Each title is subject to availability from Samuel French,
depending upon country of performance.

Acting Editions

BORN TO PERFORM

Playscripts designed from the ground up to work the way you do in rehearsal, performance and study

---

Larger, clearer text for easier reading

Wider margins for notes

Performance features such as character and props lists, sound and lighting cues, and more

---

+ CHOOSE A SIZE AND STYLE TO SUIT YOU

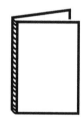

STANDARD EDITION

Our regular paperback book at our regular size

SPIRAL-BOUND EDITION

The same size as the Standard Edition, but with a sturdy, easy-to-fold, easy-to-hold spiral-bound spine

LARGE EDITION

A4 size and spiral bound, with larger text and a blank page for notes opposite every page of text. Perfect for technical and directing use

---

LEARN MORE | **samuelfrench.co.uk/actingeditions**

Other plays by NORMAN ROBBINS
published and licensed by Samuel French

Full-length plays:

A Tomb with a View
(*the first of the* Tomb Trilogy)

And Evermore Shall Be So

At the Sign of the "Crippled Harlequin"

The Borzoletti Monstrance

The Late Mrs Early

Nightmare

Practice to Deceive

Prescription For Murder

Pull The Other One

Slaughterhouse

Swan Song

Tiptoe Through the Tombstones
(*the second of the* Tomb Trilogy)

Wedding of the Year

Pantomimes:

Aladdin

Ali Baba and the Forty Thieves

Babes in the Wood

AUTHOR'S NOTE

Prepare to Meet Thy Tomb completes the trilogy of plays dealing with the murderous Tomb family's activities. Each is self-sufficient, with no knowledge needed of the other scripts, but obviously, if already acquainted with them, the audience's enjoyment will be enhanced. It was written in response to many requests for further adventures of the Tombs, as the combination of a baffling murder mystery and over-the-top characters seemed to appeal to all age brackets, world wide. However, as one can only go so far with a theme without familiarity breeding boredom, this offering brings down the final curtain on the Monument House brand of homicidal mayhem.

As before, the more skilled the performers and director, the more the watchers will enjoy themselves. Characters are pure stock, giving performers wonderful opportunities for truly bizarre characterization, whilst laughs and chills are present in equal amounts. Forget political correctness. Here is a family that play together and slay together. Gun, knife, poison, fatal injection; anything goes when the fog comes rolling in and there's much more hidden beneath the surrounding marsh than ever Mother Nature intended. Enter the house at your peril.

Norman Robbins

CHARACTERS

DRUSILLA TOMB
HECUBA TOMB
SIR BEVERLEY COMSTOCK
PHILLIPA COLLINS
DAPHNE SUMMERS
ANTHONY STRICKLAND
QUENTIN DANESWORTH
ROBERT SANDBROOKE
MIRANDA TORRENCE
CICELY VENNER

SYNOPSIS OF SCENES

The action of the play takes place in the Garden Room of Monument House Hotel and Alternative Health Farm, some fifty miles from London

ACT I

Scene One: Late Saturday afternoon in February
Scene Two: The same. An hour later

ACT II

Scene One: The same. Half-an-hour later
Scene Two: The same. An hour later

For
Hannah and Sanjay Thapa

ACT I

Scene One

The Garden Room of Monument House and Alternative Health Farm. A late Saturday afternoon in February.

The room is dominated by an immense black walnut fireplace in the centre of the rear wall. Outsize vases rest on the outer edges of the mantle. Above the mantle, a thick gold frame surrounds a badly executed painting of a very old woman, with staring eyes and thin lipped mouth which is set in a ferocious scowl. A heavily carved wooden fender protects against sparks from the log fire, and huge fire-dogs of brass with attendant implements are in position. A thick hearthrug is in front of the fender. Massive, meshed but empty, bookcases are built into the walls at each side of the fireplace. The one on the left, however, conceals a secret door that opens left, into the room. The wall, right, is dominated by enormous French windows. Thick velvet drapes hang from matching pelmets, and coffee-coloured net curtains obscure a view of overgrown shrubs outside. Upstage of the windows, a drinks table is set against the wall. On this, a decorative table lamp, several decanters, an old-fashioned soda syphon and a tray of glasses can be seen. Below the table is a comfortable winged armchair, downstage of the windows is an antique-looking cabinet, on this, another lamp, a bowl of snowdrops, and assorted knick-knacks. In the opposite wall are massive Gothic doors of black walnut, each door having a large brass knob. These double doors form the only obvious entrance into the room. When they are open, a glimpse of a wide hall can be seen. Upstage of the doors is an old-fashioned writing desk. On it are a collection of pens, a desk blotter and a bottle of ink. Writing paper, envelopes, etc., are in the drawers. An outdated internal telephone is fixed to the wall downstage of this. Downstage of the doors, and opposite the cabinet right, is a matching one. On this, is a display of unusual-looking dried flowers in bizarre shades. A huge settee occupies the centre of the room, and this is angled slightly to face downstage left. Behind it, a narrow table stands. The room is thickly carpeted. Wall lights provide an alternative to the central chandelier. Switches for both are by the doors.

When the curtain rises, the room is empty, but the lights are on and the doors are open.

After a moment, **DRUSILLA TOMB,** *a pale-faced girl of nineteen, enters, carrying a thick old-fashioned diary, which she is reading avidly. She wears a skirt, blouse and nondescript cardigan. In the pocket of this, she has a mobile phone.*

Moving behind the settee, she turns downstage, slows to a halt just below the left arm of the wing chair, and remains standing.

HECUBA *(offstage)* Drusilla? *(insistently)* Drusilla?

There is no reaction from **DRUSILLA** *who remains engrossed.*

Where are you, dear?

HECUBA TOMB *scurries into the room. She is a small, fussy woman in her sixties, with improbably blue hair twisted into a large bun, with several ornamental hair pins sticking out of it, making her look like Widow Twankey in* Aladdin. *She wears a bright, floral dress which does not suit her, and sensible flat shoes.*

Oh, there you are. *(moving behind the settee)* You might have answered. For all the notice anyone takes of me, I could have stayed in Cheltenham. I am family, you know, and deserve some recognition.

DRUSILLA *continues reading, unaware.*

(bitterly) Not that it seems to matter these days. The only ones having fun are you and Postumus. All I'm good for is cooking and cleaning and keeping the books straight. *(forcefully)* Drusilla.

DRUSILLA *glances round in surprise.*

(heavily) I'm trying to speak to you. *(noticing the diary)* What's that you're reading?

DRUSILLA Aunt Dora's diary.

HECUBA *(shocked)* Drusilla. You've no *right*. That's a private document.

DRUSILLA *(amused)* Hardly. She's been dead for over a year.

HECUBA *(primly)* That's no excuse. Well brought up young ladies do *not* read other people's diaries.

DRUSILLA This one does. And it's absolutely fascinating. Did you know an ounce of baking chocolate can kill a ten-pound dog? Especially if it's unsweetened. The chocolate, that is... not the dog.

HECUBA *(scornfully)* Don't be ridiculous.

DRUSILLA *(shrugging)* That's what she says *here*. *(displaying the diary)* And if *she* didn't know, then who did? *(sitting in the wing chair)* If you ask me, that's why she scared the family so much. She was deadlier than the rest of us put together.

She returns to her reading.

HECUBA *(shocked)* Drusilla. That's a *very* un-Christian remark. We've *all* done our best to uphold the family tradition – even outsiders like myself. How you can make such horrible

aspersions... *(her words trail away, then suddenly rallying)*
And what about Grandmother *Vesta?* You're not suggesting
she didn't...

DRUSILLA *(looking up)* Gran was a *specialist*, Aunt Hecuba.
She'd forgotten more about disposals than we'll ever *know*.
And I'm *not* casting aspersions. You've only to look in the
Family Records book to see how right I am. Aunt Dora
wiped out more people than the plague *(dreamily)* Oh, I
wish I'd known her.

HECUBA *(sniffily)* Well I *did*. And believe me, she was nothing
special. *(Moving left)* In my opinion, her cousin Athene
was *far* superior.

DRUSILLA *(curiously)* How would *you* know? You never even
met her.

HECUBA *(moving down left of the settee)* Perhaps not. But your
grandmother told me about her. *(fondly)* Such a clever lady,
Athene Tomb. Her poison-tipped hairpins were a stroke
of genius. I even wear them myself as a kind of homage.
(touching them gingerly) You should be *ashamed* of yourself,
letting her die like that. *(firmly)* If *I'd* been here—

DRUSILLA *(sharply)* You'd have ended up dead like the rest of
them. *(relenting)* It wasn't a picnic, you know. If it hadn't
been for Posti, *I'd* be down in the marsh as well.

HECUBA *(huffily)* All the same... There was no excuse for
being taken in by an amateur. *(proudly)* The Tombs are
professional killers. *(bitterly)* There ought to be a *law* against
the general public dabbling in things they know nothing
about. No wonder business is bad. We've not had a client
in *weeks*.

She sits on the settee.

DRUSILLA *(mildly)* It's a quiet time of year.

HECUBA *(tartly)* There was no such thing when Septimus ran the
business. Everyone worked round the *clock* to fulfil contracts.
(scornfully) Two years later and the house is turned into

an Alternative Health Farm – whatever *that* is – and only three of the family are left. Three. Out of *fifteen.*

Her face creases in anguish.

DRUSILLA *(gently)* That's not *my* fault, Aunt Hecuba. Six of them were killed before anyone realized what was going on – or *five* if you don't count Aunt Monica. We've still no idea what happened to *her.* And as for the others... If it hadn't been for Posti, there'd have been even *less* of us to carry on the business.

HECUBA *(huffily)* And if *I'd* been included in your grandmother's plans instead of being totally ignored, as usual, we'd most likely have avoided *any* deaths – apart from the ones who *deserved* it. *(scornfully)* But oh, no. I was only her son's *second* wife. Good for nothing but bookkeeping and making sure everyone's meals were on time. *(sharply)* Well I *have* killed before, you know. I'm not a *novice.* You've no *idea* how many people I've disposed of over the years, but does anyone recognize that? Oh, no. I'm just poor old Heckie – the general dogsbody.

DRUSILLA *(soothingly)* No, you're *not,* Heckie. You know you're not... We couldn't have managed without you during Gran's last weeks.

HECUBA *(petulantly)* That's not what *she* thought. You wouldn't *believe* how badly she treated me, sometimes. *(stiffly)* I knew she never *liked* me, of course. Just look at that bouquet on my wedding day. It was pure *luck* your Aunt Fabia picked it up before *I* did.

She rises as though to leave.

DRUSILLA *(mildly)* I'm sure it was only a *joke.*

HECUBA *(bitterly)* It didn't make me laugh. It took six of your uncles to hold her down when the convulsions started.

DRUSILLA *(pointedly)* She didn't die, though, did she?

HECUBA No. But it took weeks for that awful rash to fade. And all her hair fell out. *(hurting)* No... I was never a favourite of Vesta Tomb. *(glaring at the portrait above the mantle)* As far as she was concerned, I'd no place in the family business.

DRUSILLA Hecuba...

HECUBA *(slightly louder)* And now she's gone, you're treating me exactly the same. You didn't even discuss the changes to this place with me *(waving her arm distractedly)* before going ahead with them. *(bitterly)* If Septimus were alive today, he'd be turning in his grave. This was his library. And look at it now. Hardly a bookcase left, and as for the décor—

DRUSILLA *(patiently)* We've got to move with the times, Heckie. Twenty years ago, the world and his wife didn't have mobile phones and computers, etc. When the family disposed of someone, no one suspected a thing. Most of Aunt Dora's poisons were so far off the scale it never crossed anyone's mind that the deaths were anything but natural. And as for Uncle Lucien—

HECUBA *(tartly)* There's little in the history of the Tomb family I'm unaware of, Drusilla. I can recite their achievements in my sleep. As my book on the subject will shortly prove.

DRUSILLA *(surprised)* Book?

HECUBA *(primly)* It was my surprise for your grandmother's hundredth birthday. I foolishly thought it might change her attitude toward me. But now that that problem's resolved itself, it'll have to suffice as a simple testament to a unique English family.

DRUSILLA *(alarmed)* You can't publish a book about us.

HECUBA *(coldly)* Do give me some credit, Drusilla. Now Vesta's gone—

There is a heavy pounding at the main door, off left.

(startled) Who's that?

She gazes off into the hall.

DRUSILLA *(puzzled)* How should I know? We're not expecting anyone, are we?

HECUBA Not that I know of. *(remembering)* Unless it's Miss Venner.

DRUSILLA *(frowning)* And what would she want here?

HECUBA She is the family solicitor.

DRUSILLA *(correcting her)* Not any more. The minute Gran moved in here, she severed all connections with Penworthy, Venner and Crayle. If it hadn't been for them, none of the family would have died.

HECUBA *(firmly)* Well I like her. And in my opinion, Vesta was quite unfair. They'd handled our business for two hundred years and poor Cicely was devastated when Vesta made those awful allegations.

DRUSILLA *(grimly)* Not half as much as we were. Between the other two, they'd wiped out most of the family.

The knocking comes again.

You'd better answer it. But if it is Cicely Venner, you can send her away again PDQ.

HECUBA *(huffily)* I'll do no such thing, Drusilla. In case you've forgotten, I still own a third of Tomb Enterprises, and if I wish to invite my friends inside, I most certainly shall.

HECUBA *sweeps out.*

DRUSILLA *sighs heavily and returns to her reading.*

There is a short silence, then HECUBA*'s voice is heard.*

HECUBA *(offstage; grandly)* May I help you?

SIR BEVERLEY *(offstage; harshly)* Never mind the pleasantries. Where is she?

DRUSILLA *looks up with a frown.*

HECUBA *(offstage)* I beg your pardon.

SIR BEVERLEY *(offstage)* The old bag you work for.

HECUBA *(offstage; alarmed)* No. You can't. Come back. *(calling shrilly)* Drusilla. Drusilla.

DRUSILLA *stands.*

SIR BEVERLEY COMSTOCK *angrily enters the room. He is an aggressive north-country-born man in his sixties, expensively dressed in a dark suit and overcoat.*

SIR BEVERLEY *(glancing around swiftly, then focusing on DRUSILLA)* So where's she hiding herself?

DRUSILLA *(calmly)* I'm sorry?

HECUBA *appears in the doorway looking flushed.*

SIR BEVERLEY *(acidly)* Your double-crossing grandmother, by the look of it. Athene bloody Tomb.

HECUBA *(startled)* Athene?

Her hand flies to her throat.

SIR BEVERLEY *(ignoring her)* We've something to discuss, me and her, and I don't want any excuses. If she's not here in two minutes flat, it's the last mistake she'll ever make.

DRUSILLA *(calmly)* And do you have a name, Mr...?

SIR BEVERLEY *(coldly)* Comstock. Sir Beverley Comstock.

HECUBA *(startled)* Not *the* Sir Beverley Comstock?

He glances at her, sourly.

DRUSILLA *(cutting in)* And why, exactly, are you looking for Aunt Athene?

SIR BEVERLEY *(sharply)* That's none of your concern. Just tell her I'm here and I'm not very happy about it.

He sniffs suspiciously and glances round.

DRUSILLA *(moving downstage right and dropping the diary onto the armchair)* That might be a problem. She's no longer with us, you see.

SIR BEVERLEY Then where is she?

HECUBA *(moving into the room)* With the rest of the family, of course. Down in the—

DRUSILLA *(turning swiftly to face him)* South of France.

HECUBA *looks surprised.*

(smiling easily) And won't be back for some time. *(brightly)* But we're fully qualified to deal with problems during her absence. *(to* HECUBA*)* Aren't we, Heckie?

SIR BEVERLEY *(harshly)* The only problem I have is half a million pounds paid out and nothing to show for it.

He sniffs again.

DRUSILLA *(calmly)* Then if you'd care to sit down, *(indicating the settee)* I'll do my best to help.

SIR BEVERLEY *(rudely)* I'm looking for the organ grinder. Not her bloody monkey.

HECUBA *looks outraged.*

DRUSILLA *(unfazed)* I may be only her "monkey", Sir Beverley, but I think you'll find I'm quite capable of fulfilling any of Aunt Athene's commitments. Please.

She indicates the settee again.

SIR BEVERLEY *glowers at her for a moment, then moves around and sits.*

May I offer you a drink?

SIR BEVERLEY *(scowling)* I'm teetotal.

HECUBA *(spitefully sweet)* A nice cup of herbal tea, then? I've a lovely oleander leaf...

DRUSILLA *(warningly)* Hecuba.

HECUBA *glowers at her.*

(to SIR BEVERLEY*)* So. About your agreement with Aunt Athene?

She sits in the armchair and puts the diary on the arm right.

SIR BEVERLEY *(harshly)* My agreement was that in exchange for half a million pounds, Comstock Enterprises would find a certain thorn in its side had been extracted without any fuss, and disposed of safely.

DRUSILLA *(frowning)* Could you perhaps be a little more specific?

SIR BEVERLEY *(flatly)* I could. But you'll get nothing more till I know exactly who you two are and what this place is.

DRUSILLA Of course. I'm sorry. I should have introduced myself. Drusilla Tomb... Joint owner of the Monument House complex, with Aunt Hecuba, *(indicating her)* and my half-brother, Postumus.

SIR BEVERLEY *(scowling)* Who?

DRUSILLA Postumus. Most of the family have early Roman forenames. It's something of a tradition.

She smiles.

HECUBA *(proudly)* We're descendants of the Borgias, you see? Direct descendants.

DRUSILLA *glowers at her.*

(defiantly) Even if it's only by marriage.

SIR BEVERLEY *(ignoring her)* So where's he, then?

DRUSILLA Out on a job, I'm afraid. And may not be back for some time.

SIR BEVERLEY *(sourly)* And what's with this place? Hotel and Alternative Health Farm?

DRUSILLA *(smiling)* Basically, the family home. We've lived here since fourteen ninety-five. Though the present building's much later. Seventeen eighty-one, I believe.

HECUBA *(chipping in)* Built by Sebastian Hassock, the famous architect.

SIR BEVERLEY *(unimpressed)* Never heard of him.

HECUBA *(gushingly)* An absolute genius. And Monument House was his finest achievement. He was so proud of it, the family decided he should stay here as a permanent guest.

SIR BEVERLEY *(grunting)* I bet that thrilled him.

He sniffs the air distastefully.

HECUBA The records didn't say – but he's behind the pantry wall in the kitchen.

She realizes what she has said and covers her mouth.

SIR BEVERLEY *(distractedly)* What the hell's that smell? Is there summat wrong with your drains?

DRUSILLA It's the marsh, I'm afraid. We don't notice it ourselves.

SIR BEVERLEY *(sarcastically)* Hardly a selling point for a bloody health farm. It's enough to set off an asthma attack.

DRUSILLA *(innocently)* Do you have asthma, Sir Beverley?

SIR BEVERLEY *(sharply)* What's it to do with you?

DRUSILLA We could offer assistance if you'd any need for it. Uncle Lucien was a chemist and our own dispensary's just down the corridor.

SIR BEVERLEY *(sourly)* I'll stick to Harley Street, if you don't mind.

DRUSILLA Then back to your problem, Sir Beverley...

SIR BEVERLEY *(gazing at her thoughtfully, then coming to a decision; deliberately)* I may be wealthy, Miss Tomb, but I don't throw money round like water. When I pay for a job, I want it done with no messing about. You don't get where I am today by tolerating incompetence.

DRUSILLA *nods, but is silent.*

In November last year, I paid half a million pounds to ensure Comstock Enterprises wouldn't be taken over by a jumped-up computer company with eyes bigger than its belly. Since that day, there's not been a bloody word, and the shareholders are seriously considering an offer that'll cost me billions. What I want to know – and quickly – is how long I have to wait to have something done?

DRUSILLA *(picking up the diary and rising)* Why don't you stay for dinner, Sir Beverley? I'll make a few enquiries and have an answer for you within the hour. *(hesitating)* There's just one thing, though.

SIR BEVERLEY *(scowling)* Yes?

DRUSILLA *(curious)* How did you make contact with Aunt Athene?

SIR BEVERLEY *(flatly)* We're long-time customers, of course. Company's been using the Tomb family's services for the past eighty years or so. Last time was just before Septimus died, and if you don't mind my saying so, ladies, I'm not too impressed with the present set-up.

HECUBA *bridles.*

When he were alive, disposals were taken care of before the ink on the contract had time to dry. We'd no need to waste time chasing round the countryside looking for assurances.

DRUSILLA And how did you find the house? We've never disclosed its locality to clients.

SIR BEVERLEY *(smirking)* There's a big difference between me and my late father. I'm not in the habit of handing large sums of money to any Tom, Dick and Harriet, who think they can pull the wool over my eyes. When Athene Tomb left Comstock Tower last November, I had her followed.

HECUBA *(shocked)* Of all the deceitful...

SIR BEVERLEY *(ignoring her)* One of my detectives joined her on the Norwich train and saw her leaving it a few miles from here – at Hag's Hollow.

HECUBA *(petulantly)* Haslow. It's pronounced Haslow.

SIR BEVERLEY *(still ignoring her)* So jumping out after her, he text'd me to say where he was and assure me she'd not be out of his sight for a second.

DRUSILLA *(mildly)* I see.

SIR BEVERLEY *(sourly)* But apparently, he weren't as sharp as he thought he were. He vanished completely and hasn't been heard of since.

He stares at her.

DRUSILLA *(frowning)* You don't think we'd anything to do with it?

SIR BEVERLEY *(drily)* I did consider the matter. I don't like coincidences. But deciding to give you benefit of the doubt, I sent another one along to pick up the trail. It took a few days, but this time, he came up with the goods. *(in a satisfied manner)* Monument House.

HECUBA *(bitterly)* You should congratulate him.

SIR BEVERLEY *(scowling)* There's nothing I'd like better. But it so happens he's gone missing, too.

DRUSILLA *and* HECUBA *exchange looks.*

As Lady Bracknell might have said. To lose one detective may be regarded as a misfortune; to lose two is pretty damned suspicious.

DRUSILLA *(easily)* Well, they're nothing to do with us, Sir Beverley. But if you knew where we were, why has it taken so long to contact us?

SIR BEVERLEY *(sarcastically)* It may come as a shock, Miss Tomb, but I do have a company to run. *(harshly)* And these past few months I've been round the world twice trying to save it. The agreement was, by the time I got back, there'd be nothing more to worry about. Yet what do I find? The nominee's still breathing down my neck, I'm half a million out of pocket, and in six days' time I look like being a bloody has-been. Does that answer your question?

He gives a spluttering cough.

DRUSILLA Just leave it to me, Sir Beverley. The Tombs have always honoured their agreements. I'll have a word with Posti, and it'll all be taken care of before the weekend.

SIR BEVERLEY *(glowering)* It had better be. Because if I go down, I'll make damned sure that you lot'll go down with me. I've enough up here *(tapping his temple)* to put you away for good.

He coughs again and fumbles in his pocket for his inhaler.

HECUBA *looks venomous as he doses himself.*

DRUSILLA *(calmly)* As I said... I'll speak to Posti.

HECUBA *(frowning)* But we don't know where he is.

DRUSILLA *(soothingly)* I have his mobile number. Just find a room for Sir Beverley and see he has everything he needs. *(to SIR BEVERLEY)* I presume you'd like to freshen up before dinner?

SIR BEVERLEY *(rising and replacing his inhaler)* You'd better let Strickland know. He's out in the car.

DRUSILLA Strickland???

SIR BEVERLEY *(dismissively)* My new PA, chauffeur's off sick, so he drove me here. Bit of a wimp, but he's got his uses.

DRUSILLA I'll let him know, myself. *(to* **HECUBA***)* Aunt Hecuba?

HECUBA *(to* **SIR BEVERLEY***; glowering)* I'll put you in the Hemlock Room. It overlooks the marsh.

HECUBA *moves huffily out of the room, followed by* **SIR BEVERLEY**.

DRUSILLA *drops the diary on the table behind the settee. She takes a mobile phone out of her cardigan pocket and turns away from the door punching out a number.*

DRUSILLA *(lowering her voice)* Posti. You need to get back here. We may have a problem... Where are you? ... *(incredulously)* Where? ...Since when? *(amused)* Then what's going on? I thought you were going to... *(frowning)* I see. So how do you want me to play it? ... *(nodding at what is being said)* Heckie? Oh, being a pain as usual. Thinks we're not giving her a chance to prove her worth... *(smiling)* You have to be joking. We couldn't risk turning her loose. We'd be finished in no time. But don't worry. I'll have a word with her. Make sure she—

PHILLIPA *(offstage left; calling)* Yoo-hoo? Is anybody there?

DRUSILLA *spins to face the door, startled.*

Reception? *(brightly)* Ting-a-ling-a-li-ing?

DRUSILLA *(calling)* Coming. *(into the phone)* I'll speak to you later.

She ends the conversation and thrusts the phone into her pocket.

PHILLIPA COLLINS *appears in the doorway. She is in her forties, slightly bossy and gushing in manner. She is flamboyantly dressed for travelling and appears rather flustered.*

PHILLIPA *(crossing to* **DRUSILLA***)* Oh, thank goodness we spotted your sign. Well, Daphne did. I was too busy trying to keep the car on the road. It's years since we ran into fog and it wasn't even forecast. *(holding out her hand)* Phillipa Collins. The novelist.

DRUSILLA *(blankly)* Collins?

PHILLIPA *(hastily)* Oh, we don't have reservations, so if you can't fit us in we can go elsewhere. *(earnestly)* But we'd feel so much safer if you can manage it. I'm sure you've got excellent security. *(lowering her voice)* We've had a fright, you see.

DAPHNE SUMMERS *appears in the doorway behind her. She is in her late fifties. Small, plain, short-sighted and of a nervous disposition, she is warmly wrapped against the cold.*

DRUSILLA I'm sorry...

DAPHNE *(plaintively)* I said they wouldn't have room, Phillipa. I said they wouldn't. We'd better call the police.

PHILLIPA *(turning to DAPHNE)* And make fools of ourselves if it isn't him?

DAPHNE *(crossing to PHILLIPA; protesting)* But he followed us, Phillipa. All the way from Latchingdon.

PHILLIPA *(reassuringly)* It could have been coincidence. No one said he had a car, did they?

DAPHNE *(worried)* But he has to have. How else could he leave the bodies?

DRUSILLA *(blankly)* Bodies?

DAPHNE Of all the women he's strangled.

DRUSILLA *(baffled)* I'm sorry. I don't know what you're talking about.

DAPHNE The man in the papers. The Norfolk Strangler.

PHILLIPA You must have heard of him. You're living right on his doorstep.

DRUSILLA *(carefully)* We're a bit remote – as you've noticed. We don't have newspaper delivery.

DAPHNE *(voice rising)* But you must have television. It's been on the news for weeks. Nine poor women. All strangled and left at the side of the road.

DRUSILLA *(pretending concern)* How awful. But as I said, we're a little out of touch with the outside world. It's been months since we last had visitors.

PHILLIPA *(sympathetically)* Oh. Business not too good, then?

DRUSILLA *(realizing)* Oh. No. No. *(improvising)* That's what's been keeping us busy. We're in the middle of a conversion and we're not quite ready for opening, yet. Perhaps by the end of next month.

She smiles.

PHILLIPA *(dismayed)* So you can't accommodate us?

DRUSILLA *(with fake regret)* I'm afraid not. *(helpfully)* But I'm sure you'll find a Bed and Breakfast in Haslow. It's only a few miles down the road.

DAPHNE *(anxiously)* But what if he's still outside? Waiting for us.

PHILLIPA *(putting on a brave face)* Not very likely, Daffs. *(attempting to reason)* I mean...we don't even know he was the Strangler, do we? We could have been letting imagination run riot. *(brightly)* And even if it was him, we must have lost him in the fog. He couldn't have seen us turn in here. Whoever he was, he'll be miles away by now.

ANTHONY STRICKLAND *appears in the doorway. He is in his late twenties, on the timid side and his round, horn-rimmed spectacles give him an owlish appearance. He wears a dark suit.*

ANTHONY *(hesitantly)* Excuse me.

PHILLIPA *and* DAPHNE *give little shrieks and turn to see him.*

(weakly) I'm looking for Sir Beverley.

DRUSILLA *(recovering herself)* Mr – Strickland, is it?

ANTHONY *(relieved)* That's right. Sir Beverley's PA. There's an urgent call for him on the car phone. But the signal's playing up. I keep losing it.

DRUSILLA *(grimacing)* It is a bit of a dead spot. We even have problems with the landline. But if you'll wait here, I'll get him for you. If he's quick, he might just be lucky. *(moving to the door, then remembering the two women and turning back)* Best of luck in the village.

DRUSILLA *exits.*

ANTHONY *(apologetically)* Sorry if I startled you. There was no one on the desk.

PHILLIPA *(embarrassed)* We thought you were the Norfolk Strangler.

DAPHNE *(faintly)* He's been following us ever since we left the tearoom.

ANTHONY *looks at them oddly.*

PHILLIPA She means we think he's been following us. He's certainly been behind us for the last half-hour. Couldn't shake him off no matter which way we turned. She was quite worried, *(to DAPHNE)* weren't you, Daffs?

DAPHNE *(nodding)* He was trying to make us stop. Flashing his lights and tooting his horn like a maniac. It was quite frightening. He was so close at one point we could even see his face.

PHILLIPA Heaven knows what he was screaming about, but I wasn't pulling up to find out. As soon as we ran into fog, I turned down the first side road and straight into this place when Daphne spotted the sign.

ANTHONY *(moving to behind the settee)* Have you called the police?

PHILLIPA *(shaking her head)* I think we're safe, now. And it might have been simply road rage. You know how some men are? Can't bear to see a woman behind the wheel. Especially if she's driving a Rolls-Royce Phantom. Must threaten their masculinity, or something. Still...there's no harm done. And we don't want any unpleasantness spoiling things. All we need's a little rest and recreation.

DAPHNE To re-charge her batteries. *(proudly)* Phillipa's a writer, you see. Really gory murder mysteries.

PHILLIPA *(trying to silence her)* Daphne.

ANTHONY *(interested)* Oh. *(to* PHILLIPA*)* Are you famous, then?

PHILLIPA *(embarrassed)* I wouldn't say famous.

DAPHNE *(protesting)* But you are, Phillipa. You've written dozens of books. *(to* ANTHONY*)* She outsells Caro French and Ermyntrude Ash.

ANTHONY *looks blank.*

PHILLIPA *(acidly)* Hardly a recommendation, dear. Ash is dead, and the last I heard of French, she'd been remaindered at Glasgow airport. *(to* ANTHONY*)* It was supposed to be a secret. As far as my publishers know, I'm out in Africa, researching my next book. If they hear I'm in Norfolk, they'll be wanting me for signings and God knows what else. Please don't let on you've seen me here.

ANTHONY *(hastily)* Of course not. I wouldn't dream of it. *(awkwardly)* But should I ask for your autograph?

PHILLIPA *(drily)* I don't think that'd impress anyone, dear. *(brightly)* But how about a signed copy of *The Seventh Glass Dagger*? If you'd like to come back to the car with us, I'll give you a copy.

ANTHONY That's very kind of you, but I'm not much of a reader. Haven't the time, really. *(bashfully)* Looking after Sir Beverley.

PHILLIPA Keeps you on your toes, does he? Still...all work and no play, you know. *(to* **DAPHNE***)* Come on, Daffs. Better be off before the fog gets any thicker. The last thing we want is to end up in a boggy ditch, smack in the middle of nowhere.

ANTHONY Going far, are you?

PHILLIPA Haven't a clue. We've not booked in anywhere, so we're free agents. We'll just press on till we find somewhere with a couple of spare rooms.

ANTHONY Then why not stay here? It is a hotel. *(glancing round)* Sort of.

PHILLIPA Not open yet. According to the girl.

DAPHNE Not till next month. *(sniffing unhappily)* And they must get their drains seen to.

ANTHONY *(protesting)* But there must be some rooms ready. And it is getting worse out there. You can't see your hand in front of you. I was going to mention it to Sir Beverley. If his meeting doesn't end soon, we'll have to stay ourselves. He won't want to travel in this.

PHILLIPA *(glancing round the room)* I don't know. It's a bit on the creepy side. Not what we expected when we spotted the sign.

ANTHONY *(wryly)* Yes. It is a bit Gothic-looking. But it's probably steeped in history. If only walls could speak, eh?

QUENTIN DANESWORTH *enters the room like a tornado. He is an effeminate man in his late sixties, portly, but expensively and flamboyantly dressed, with expressive features and given to over-elaborate gestures.*

QUENTIN *(gushingly)* Oh, but they can, dear boy. They most certainly can. And I'm just the person who can tell you what they're saying. *(simpering)* Quentin Danesworth, at your service.

He gives a theatrical bow.

DAPHNE *(surprised)* Not the television man? Danesworth's Domiciles?

QUENTIN *(happily)* One and the same, dear lady. One and the same. You're a fan, of course? Isn't everyone? The most successful historical show on television today, and all my own idea. *(gazing around the room in delight)* But this, *(waving his arms)* this...will send the ratings rocketing... *(ecstatically)* The lost house of Sebastian Hassock. And I'm the one who found it. *(preening, then remembering)* You do give permission to film here, of course? With substantial remuneration to cover any inconvenience.

He beams coyly.

PHILLIPA *(hastily)* I'm afraid you've made a mistake.

QUENTIN *(sharply)* Oh, I never make mistakes, dear lady. The name of Danesworth is a by word for accuracy, reliability and tenacity. Without question, the house was built by Sebastian Hassock in, or around seventeen eighty-one, and I have the papers to prove it.

ANTHONY Papers?

QUENTIN Oh, yes. For many years, I've researched all Hassock's buildings, demolished or otherwise. *(moving down left)* Every diary, every scrap of paper referring to his achievements is now in my possession *(proudly)* and I can truthfully say that no man alive knows more about his work than I do. *(preening)* But of course, like myself, he had his little secrets. *(simpering)* After designing and building the Great Abattoir in Butcher's Row, he drew up plans for a massive country house, complete with secret passages, hidden rooms and its own private vaults. A house such as England had never seen before. *(with great drama)* But shortly afterwards, he and his plans vanished without trace and the location of his final masterpiece was lost to human ken.

He strikes a tragic pose.

PHILLIPA So what makes you think it was this one?

QUENTIN *(pityingly)* My dear lady. Just look at it. The plasterwork. The design. The layout. It simply screams of Hassock. It's the most exciting find of the century.

ANTHONY *(looking round)* I can't see any secret passages.

DAPHNE Or hidden rooms.

QUENTIN *(chuckling)* But they're there, my darlings, and that's the beauty of Hassock's design. You could hide an army within these seemingly solid walls.

He sits on the settee.

PHILLIPA *(overwhelmed)* Fancy. *(pulling herself together)* Well... it's been nice meeting you, Mr Danesworth, but we'd better be off. Come along, Daphne.

She moves towards the door.

QUENTIN *(startled)* But what about my programme?

PHILLIPA We'll look forward to seeing it.

PHILLIPA *exits, followed by* DAPHNE.

QUENTIN *(rising in agitation)* Wait. Wait.

He moves as though to follow them.

ANTHONY You don't have to worry. They're not the owners. They're just a couple who've lost their way.

QUENTIN *(turning back; annoyed)* You mean I've wasted my time on a pair of nobodies?

ANTHONY *(helpfully)* One of them's a writer.

QUENTIN *(peeved)* Writer. Shmiter. *(suddenly aghast)* Oh, my God. I've just told them why I'm here. If the news gets out before I've done the programme, the place'll be crawling with paparazzi.

PHILLIPA *and* DAPHNE *hurry back into the room.*

PHILLIPA *(gasping)* He's here. He's here. Getting out of his car.

She attempts to hide behind **ANTHONY**.

DAPHNE *(in a panic)* The Norfolk Strangler.

She joins her.

QUENTIN *(putting his hands to his cheeks in horror)* Oh, my God.

ROBERT *(offstage)* Is anybody there? Hallo?

PHILLIPA, DAPHNE *and* **QUENTIN** *begin to scream hysterically.*

ROBERT SANDBROOKE *appears in the doorway. He is in his late thirties, wearing a tweed jacket with a mobile phone in the pocket, polo neck sweater and designer jeans. He stares at them in bewilderment.*

ANTHONY *(snatching up the soda syphon)* One step closer and I'll... *(desperately)* squirt it.

He takes aim.

ROBERT *(incredulously)* Are you lot barmy?

The trio stop screaming.

All I want's my laptop back.

PHILLIPA *(blankly)* Laptop?

ROBERT *(tightly)* You picked up mine by mistake. In the café. Yours is in the back of my car. I've been following you for miles.

DAPHNE *(weakly)* You mean...you're not the Norfolk Strangler?

ROBERT *looks puzzled.*

(hopefully) You're not going to kill us?

ROBERT *(baffled)* Do I look like I'm going to kill anyone? I want my laptop back, that's all. So if you wouldn't mind... I'd like to collect what I came for and carry on with my honeymoon.

QUENTIN *(surprised)* Honeymoon? You're on your honeymoon?

ROBERT *(glaring at him)* Some of us are still normal, believe it or not.

QUENTIN *(offended)* Oooh. Excuse me for breathing.

He sits on the settee again.

ROBERT *(to* **PHILLIPA***)* My laptop?

PHILLIPA *(flustered)* I'll get it for you now. I'm terribly sorry. I'd no idea.

DAPHNE *(suspiciously)* How do we know he's telling the truth? How do we know you got the wrong laptop? It could be the way he tricked the others.

ROBERT *(irritated)* What others?

DAPHNE *(fearfully)* The ones you killed and left in the lay-bys.

ROBERT *(tiredly)* For crying out loud... *(firmly)* I'm Robert Sandbrooke, doing Norfolk for the first time in my life, and trying to begin my honeymoon.

MIRANDA TORRENCE *enters. She is in her early forties, a stunning, artificial blonde with a pneumatic figure who slinks around like a panther stalking its prey. Unfortunately her IQ seems very much in question. She wears a skin-tight, low-cut black dress beneath a long fake-fur coat.*

MIRANDA *(in a "little girl" voice)* Is something wrong, Bobby?

The trio gape at her.

ROBERT *(sighing)* Miranda. I told you to stay out of sight.

MIRANDA *(pouting)* But it's cold out there. And besides...I like the look of this place. Why can't we stay here instead of going to Norwich?

ROBERT *(peeved)* Because we've a suite booked at the Royal, in case you'd forgotten.

MIRANDA But this looks much more interesting.

PHILLIPA *(recovering herself)* I'm afraid you're out of luck, Mrs...Sandbrooke. It's not open yet. The nearest place is Halso, or something. About seven miles away.

MIRANDA *(plaintively)* But they wouldn't turn us away on a night like this. It's our wedding night. I'm sure they'd find room for us.

DAPHNE *(bridling)* Why should they? They've not given us any choice. And we were here first.

ANTHONY *(hastily)* I'm sure there'd be room for everyone if it came to it. *(replacing the syphon)* I mean...the place must be full of beds, open or not.

ROBERT *(firmly)* We'll take our chances with the fog. And besides...it smells like an open drain in here. *(to PHILLIPA)* Now if you wouldn't mind?

PHILLIPA *(remembering)* Oh, yes. Yes. Of course.

MIRANDA *gives a pathetic and obviously false cough and clutches at her throat.*

ROBERT *(concerned)* What is it?

MIRANDA *(weakly)* My throat. It's hurting. It must be the fog.

She coughs again.

ROBERT *(worried)* Oh, my God. *(hurrying to her)* I'll call a doctor.

He gets his mobile phone out.

MIRANDA *(hastily)* No, no, darling. I'll just sit next to this gentleman *(indicating QUENTIN)* till I'm feeling better. *(pathetically)* I don't want to make a fuss.

ROBERT *(guiding her round the back of the settee)* I told you to stay in the car. I said I wouldn't be long.

MIRANDA *(weakly)* But I couldn't bear you being out of my sight. Not today of all days.

She sits on the left of the settee.

QUENTIN *winces and edges away from her.*

PHILLIPA *(unconvinced)* Perhaps a glass of water might help?

ROBERT *(scornfully)* Miranda drinks nothing but champagne. She has to take care of her voice.

ANTHONY *(interested)* Oh. *(to her)* Are you a singer, then?

ROBERT *(glaring at him)* Do you watch television, Mr whatever your name is?

ANTHONY *(taken aback)* Haven't the time, really. Sir Beverley keeps me busy.

ROBERT *(pityingly)* Then it may have escaped your notice that my wife is Miranda Torrence. The actress.

No one reacts to this.

(pointedly) She does the voice for "Purple-Green Pony" in *Pansy's Magic Turnip Field.*

MIRANDA *attempts to look modest.*

PHILLIPA *(blankly)* Purple-Green Pony????

ANTHONY No wonder she's a little hoarse.

He titters.

ROBERT *glares at him and he falls silent.*

HECUBA *enters.*

HECUBA We'll be dining in fifteen min— *(realizing there are others in the room)* Who are you? *(anxiously)* What are you doing here?

PHILLIPA *(soothingly)* We were looking for accommodation. But apparently you're not open yet.

HECUBA *(suspiciously)* Who said so? Who told you that?

DAPHNE The girl who was in here when we arrived.

HECUBA *(sharply)* Then you've no right to stay when you've not been invited. This is my home and I won't have it over-run by strangers.

ROBERT *(harshly)* Well, don't worry on our account. I'll just collect my property and we'll be leaving. Come on, Miranda.

MIRANDA *rises and turns towards* HECUBA, *who takes a shocked step backwards and clutches at her throat.* MIRANDA *looks puzzled.*

ANTHONY *(frowning)* Is something wrong?

HECUBA *(recovering herself)* No...no. It's just for a moment I thought...she was someone else. *(firmly)* Now please leave. All of you.

All but ANTHONY *prepare to leave.*

QUENTIN *(rising)* If I might have a moment, Mrs Tomb? It's about your beautiful house.

HECUBA *(blankly)* House?

QUENTIN *(turning on the charm)* You are, of course, aware this magnificent building was designed and built by the great Sebastian Hassock in—

HECUBA *(cutting in)* Seventeen eighty-one.

QUENTIN *(beaming)* Precisely. And until today, not a... *(realizing)* You do know?

HECUBA *(tartly)* Why shouldn't I? *(firmly)* I know more about this house than anyone alive.

QUENTIN *(smirking)* Without wishing to be rude, Mrs Tomb, I sincerely doubt that. I've spent the last forty years of my life studying Hassock's designs and know every nook and cranny of his unique buildings. The secret rooms, hidden passages...

HECUBA *(faintly)* Passages?

QUENTIN Behind every wall. *(archly)* You did know about them, didn't you?

HECUBA *(recovering herself)* No, I didn't. And neither do you. If there were anything like that in this house, we'd have known about it long ago. It's been in the family since the day it was built.

QUENTIN *(smugly)* Then allow me to demonstrate.

He scuttles round the settee and up to the bookcase left of the fireplace, fingers searching a section of its frame.

HECUBA *(alarmed)* What are you doing?

The bookcase pivots, revealing a darkened recess. The others react in amazement and HECUBA *is frozen to the spot.*

QUENTIN *(triumphantly)* Voilà.

He gestures at the opening and takes a bow.

PHILLIPA Oh, my goodness.

ANTHONY *(gaping)* A priest's hole.

QUENTIN *(beaming)* Not at all, dear boy. It's much, much more than that. From this opening you can reach any part of the house without a soul seeing or hearing you. Would you care to explore with me?

ANTHONY *(doubtfully)* It's a bit on the dark side.

QUENTIN *(pulling out his key ring to which a small torch is attached)* Which is why I always carry a light. *(brandishing it)* Though I've certainly done my share of groping in the dark, if you'll excuse the expression. *(smirking)* Shall I lead?

QUENTIN *vanishes into the opening.*

ANTHONY *looks at* HECUBA, *who has not moved. Seeing no reaction, he cautiously enters the passageway and vanishes from sight.*

PHILLIPA *begins to follow him.*

DAPHNE *(grabbing at* PHILLIPA *in alarm)* No, Phillipa.

PHILLIPA *(excitedly)* Don't be a wuss, Daffy. *(pulling free)* I can use this in a book. Come on.

PHILLIPA *exits into the passage and vanishes.*

(offstage) Wait for us.

Reluctantly, DAPHNE *follows and vanishes.*

MIRANDA Bobby?

ROBERT *(firmly)* You must be joking.

MIRANDA *(pouting)* But I've never been in a secret passage before.

ROBERT I don't like confined spaces. Especially dark ones.

MIRANDA I'll hold your hand.

She flutters her lashes at him.

ROBERT *(reluctantly)* Well, not too far, then.

They enter the passage and vanish.

HECUBA *remains motionless, staring at the opening.*

DRUSILLA *enters and takes in the scene.*

DRUSILLA *(puzzled)* What's happened? Why's the bookcase open?

HECUBA *(dazedly)* I couldn't stop him. He knew where it was.

DRUSILLA Who did? What are you talking about?

HECUBA *(wildly)* The man. He opened the bookcase and showed them all.

DRUSILLA *(impatiently)* All who? For goodness sake, talk sense.

HECUBA The room. It was full of strangers when I came in. They've all gone into the passage with him.

DRUSILLA Oh, my God. *(staring at it)* Where did they come from?

HECUBA I don't know. I was in the kitchen. *(suddenly)* But Posti—

DRUSILLA *(cutting in)* —'s got other things on his mind, at present. *(moving down left)* We'll deal with this ourselves.

HECUBA So what are we going to do?

DRUSILLA *(firmly)* Exactly what the family's always done. Make quite sure that none of them leaves here alive.

HECUBA *gives a delighted smile.*

Blackout.

Scene Two

An hour later. The room is as before but the secret panel is closed. After a moment, PHILLIPA *enters, followed by* DAPHNE. *Both are minus their outdoor clothing and carry their handbags.*

PHILLIPA Well it's not exactly the Savoy, but the meal wasn't bad. For a health farm.

DAPHNE And we don't have to worry about finding rooms for the night, do we? We couldn't have carried on. Not with the fog the way it is. It's thicker than ever.

PHILLIPA *(moving behind the wing chair to peer out of the windows)* The thing is, what are we going to do for the next few hours? It's too early for bed, and I don't fancy sitting around watching the lovebirds billing and cooing. *(turning away with a frown)* Where are they, by the way? There wasn't a sign of them at dinner.

DAPHNE Perhaps they had room service?

PHILLIPA *(unconvinced)* Hmm. *(looking at the bookcase)* We could take another look behind that, I suppose. See where it does lead.

DAPHNE *(unhappily)* I'd rather we didn't, Phillipa. You heard what Mrs Tomb said?

PHILLIPA *(looking at her askance)* That it might be dangerous? *(grunting scornfully)* Looked safe as houses to me. Bit dusty, but that was it. We could have explored for ages if you hadn't screamed like that and made him drop his torch. I thought you were being murdered.

She sits in the wing chair.

DAPHNE *(defensively)* Something touched me.

PHILLIPA *(drily)* Probably a spiderweb. But if he sues you for a new torch bulb, don't come crying to me.

DAPHNE *(moving down and sitting on the settee)* We could play cards. I've a pack in my suitcase.

PHILLIPA I'm not in the mood for "Old Maid", Daff. I want to be doing something. *(brightening)* If I made a few notes, I could use it as a setting, couldn't I?

DAPHNE *(frowning)* What?

PHILLIPA *(impatiently)* This place. It'd be perfect for my next book. *(with relish)* Swirling fog. Secret passages. Bodies left, right and centre.

DAPHNE *(pained)* Phillipa. You're supposed to be on holiday.

PHILLIPA *(acidly)* Yes. In Darkest Africa. Why did I let you drag me here? It's about as much fun as haemorrhoids.

She puts her handbag beside her.

DAPHNE *(protesting)* It wasn't my idea. I suggested Cornwall. You were the one who decided on Norfolk.

PHILLIPA *(firmly)* Then you should have talked me out of it. *(relenting)* Still...if I can work something up about this place, it could be a blessing in disguise. *(thoughtfully)* Do you think the old girl'd make a good killer? I could see her dishing out poisoned Chianti, couldn't you?

DAPHNE *(disapprovingly)* She's not at all like a killer. *(fondly)* She reminds me of my grandmother.

PHILLIPA *(brightly)* Exactly. And that's why she'd be perfect. Who'd suspect a dotty old woman of bumping people off? *(glancing round)* Get me something to write on, will you? I've got an idea.

She fumbles in her handbag.

DAPHNE *looks round vaguely, then rises, moves to the desk and cautiously opens a drawer to look inside.*

HECUBA *enters and sees her.*

HECUBA *(indignantly)* Excuse me. That happens to be private property.

DAPHNE *(mortified)* I'm terribly sorry.

She closes the drawer and backs away.

HECUBA *(icily)* How dare you pry into things that don't concern you? It's an absolute outrage.

PHILLIPA *(rising hastily)* Don't blame her, Mrs Tomb. It's my fault. I'm plotting a new book, you see, and I wanted some paper to make notes.

DAPHNE *(helpfully)* About this place.

PHILLIPA *(soothingly)* It'd make a wonderful setting for a murder mystery.

HECUBA *(frostily)* I don't approve of murder mysteries. They always end badly.

DAPHNE *(puzzled)* But the killers get caught.

HECUBA *(tartly)* Exactly. Quite unrealistic. If I wrote a murder mystery, no one would ever know who'd done the murder. *(firmly)* They wouldn't even know there'd been one.

PHILLIPA *(drily)* Rather defeating the object, wouldn't you think?

DAPHNE *(gushingly)* Phillipa's books sell millions. She knows more about poisons than anyone. Even Katherine John...

PHILLIPA *(tiredly)* Daffy...

DAPHNE *(protesting)* But she did, Phillipa. You showed me the letter she sent. *(to* HECUBA*)* It said "Dear Phillipa..."

PHILLIPA *(sharply)* Daphne.

DAPHNE *falls silent in shock.*

(more gently) I'm sure Mrs Tomb's got far more to do than listen to you prattling on about who writes to me. *(to* HECUBA*)* It must be awful having unexpected guests before

you've really had time to open. *(smiling)* But at least we won't bother you much longer.

HECUBA *(startled)* Who said so? *(Agitated)* How did you know?

PHILLIPA *(confused)* Well...we'll be leaving as soon as the fog lifts.

HECUBA *(realizing)* Oh. Yes. Of course. *(briskly)* But if you wouldn't mind, I'd like you to move to the Morning Room. It's just on the right, down the corridor. *(sweetly)* I'm an early riser, you see, and I must clean this room before retiring. *(briskly)* Can't have it looking like a pigsty when there's visitors about, can we? Heaven knows where the dust comes from.

She pretends to brush some away.

DAPHNE *(sympathetically)* Under the secret door, I suppose. There was a gap under my back door that let all sorts of things in till I realized and had it fixed. I was always cleaning up.

PHILLIPA *(quickly)* And speaking of doors. I know you said it could be dangerous...but I wonder if I might just have another peep into your secret passageway before we leave? *(smiling)* We can't go without finding where it leads, can we? We'd never sleep again.

HECUBA *(drily)* Oh, you'll sleep, all right. Believe me.

DAPHNE *(pleading)* She'd be ever so grateful. *(to PHILLIPA)* Wouldn't you, Phillipa?

HECUBA *(firmly)* I'll speak to Drusilla. Now if you wouldn't mind? *(She indicates the door)*

PHILLIPA *(rising)* Come on, Daffy. Let Mrs Tomb get on with her work.

PHILLIPA *and* DAPHNE *turn right and exit.*

HECUBA *glances round the room suspiciously, then follows.*

A moment later, there is a tapping sound from behind the secret panel. After a while it stops. There is silence.

MIRANDA *enters the room furtively. She has removed her coat to reveal her voluptuous figure and moves directly to the panel, running her fingers over the woodwork as though searching. The panel suddenly opens and* QUENTIN *is revealed. Both react.*

QUENTIN *(fluttering)* Miss Torrence.

MIRANDA *(confused)* Mr Danesworth.

QUENTIN *(breathlessly)* Such a fright, you gave me. *(recovering rapidly)* There I was, all alone in the darkness, and suddenly you appear. *(stepping into the room)* I hope I didn't startle you?

He minces daintily down right.

MIRANDA No. No. Of course not. I was... *(hastily)* looking for something to read.

QUENTIN *(turning to her and raising an eyebrow)* In an empty bookcase? *(wagging a bejewelled finger at her)* Naughty, naughty. If you're going to tell porkies, you must always make them convincing. *(waspishly)* I know exactly what you were up to, Miss Purple-Green Pony.

He glowers at her.

MIRANDA You do?

QUENTIN You're as excited as I am with Hassock's masterpiece. Not surprising when we're both in the same business, so to speak. *(with unexpected venom)* But let's get things straight, dear. This is my discovery, and nobody pulls a fast one on Quentin Danesworth. You'll get credit for this over my dead body.

He glowers at her.

MIRANDA *(taken aback)* I don't know what you're talking about.

QUENTIN *(waspishly)* Pull the other one, dear. You were looking for the catch that opened the panel. Go on. Admit it.

MIRANDA *(dropping the "fragile" voice)* All right. I was. But it's nothing to do with you. I couldn't care less about Hassock and his bloody house. I think I lost an earring in there, and if Bobby finds out he'll kill me. They belonged to his Great Aunt Fanny, or somebody, and have been in his family since Dick's days. I've only had them four hours.

QUENTIN *(surprised)* An earring? *(moving back to her contritely)* Oh, darling. I'm so sorry. I know just how you feel. I lost a body piercing once and thought I was going to die. Luckily it turned up in Alistair's... *(stopping short)* Well...I found it. And all ended happily. *(brightly)* So what does it look like? This earring?

MIRANDA *(improvising)* Like the other one. About this long *(indicating)* with sapphires and diamonds. It must be worth thousands.

QUENTIN *(screwing up his face in thought)* Can't say I noticed it. But then again, it's so dark in there, I could have walked on it without registering. I ran out of matches before I got to the bottom of the steps. That's why I couldn't find the catch on the other side.

MIRANDA But what were you doing in there?

QUENTIN *(waspishly)* If I'd relied on those people for permission to explore, I'd have run out of moisturiser. I wasn't leaving here without examining as much as I possibly could. *(smirking)* Luckily, I know more about this place than anybody and found another entrance in my bedroom. *(gleefully)* What a treasure this place is. It's got secrets they couldn't begin to imagine, and when my show goes on air, it'll be absolutely sensational. *(inspired)* You could even be one of my guests.

He looks at her hopefully.

MIRANDA *(sourly)* It'll make a change from Purple-Green Pony. *(hotly)* If only they knew how I hated that show. If it wasn't for the money... *(breaking off)* I'd rather do *Big Brother* or one of the other trashy "realities". *(ruefully)* To think I spent three years studying drama to play the voice of a brain-dead foam-rubber puppet.

QUENTIN *(soothingly)* But I'm sure you do it beautifully.

ROBERT'*s voice is heard off left.*

ROBERT *(offstage; calling)* Miranda, precious?

MIRANDA *(startled)* Bobby. *(agitated)* He mustn't find me here.

QUENTIN *(grabbing her arm)* Quick. Inside the passageway.

QUENTIN *and* MIRANDA *hurry inside the panel, which closes behind them.*

ROBERT *(offstage)* Are you there, darling?

ROBERT *enters left, glances round in a puzzled manner, then turns to exit again.*

DRUSILLA *appears in the doorway.*

DRUSILLA *(pointedly)* Can I help you?

ROBERT I was looking for my wife.

DRUSILLA *(entering)* Is she not in your room?

ROBERT No. She...er...came back down to collect her make-up case and I haven't seen her since.

DRUSILLA *(smiling)* Well I'm sure there's nothing to worry about. She's probably taken a wrong turning, somewhere. There's miles of corridors in Monument House, and we've not put up signs, yet. Is everything all right? You're quite comfortable?

ROBERT In the room, you mean? Oh, yes. It's fine. Fine. I've always wanted to sleep in a four-poster. But the – er – lightswitch seems to be faulty. Or the bulb's gone.

DRUSILLA Oh. I forgot to mention that. We're in the middle of rewiring and only the bedside lights are functioning at present.

ROBERT Ah. That'll be it, then. *(hastily)* But it's not a problem. We still appreciate you letting us stay the night. It's pretty bad out there.

He glances at the windows.

DRUSILLA It's the least we could do. And if there's anything you need, you've only to ask.

ROBERT Thanks. *(short silence)* Well... I – er – I'd better find Miranda.

ROBERT moves past her and exits. DRUSILLA watches him thoughtfully, then glances around the room suspiciously before exiting.

DRUSILLA *(offstage; calling)* You won't find her there, Mr Sandbrooke. It only leads to the cellars and they've not been used in years.

There is a short pause, then CICELY VENNER enters. She is a striking but hard-faced woman in her late thirties, wearing a winter coat that hangs open to reveal a smart, dark, two-piece suit and grey blouse and carrying a matching handbag. Moving to the fire, she stoops to warm her hands

A few moments later, HECUBA enters wearing latex gloves and carrying a dish of Turkish Delight. She sees CICELY's back.

HECUBA *(startled)* Oh.

CICELY turns to her.

(surprised) Cicely.

She hastily puts the dish down on the table behind the settee.

CICELY *(smiling)* Hecuba.

She moves towards her, opening her arms.

HECUBA *(flustered)* We weren't expecting you...

CICELY *(hugging her)* I know, dear, I know. But I had to warn you. I should have done it sooner but after the misunderstanding with Vesta, I wasn't sure anyone would listen.

She releases HECUBA.

HECUBA *(staunchly)* You can always rely on me, Cicely. I said so at the time. Vesta was quite wrong to sever our connections. *(proudly)* And I told her so.

CICELY *(smiling)* You're so understanding, Hecuba. *(wistfully)* If only she hadn't been so distrustful.

HECUBA *(primly)* That was Vesta, all over. Not a kind word for anyone but Posti and Drusilla. But who did she rely on to keep the accounts in order? Certainly not them. *(bitterly)* It wouldn't have hurt her to give me a little recognition.

She strips off her gloves and puts them in her pocket.

CICELY *(sympathetically)* I know, dear. I know.

HECUBA *(fuming)* And as for helping with disposals, you'd have thought I knew nothing. *(brightening)* Still...she knows better, now, doesn't she?

CICELY *looks at her, askance.*

But never mind that, dear. *(curiously)* What do you want to warn me about?

CICELY *(uncertainly)* I think the others should hear it, too.

HECUBA *(sniffily)* Oh, they'd be much too busy at present. And I'm not even sure they'd listen since Vesta finished brainwashing them.

CICELY *(considering)* Perhaps you're right. But they do need to know. And the sooner, the better.

HECUBA Then why don't you sit and tell me?

She indicates the settee.

CICELY *moves to the settee and sits right.* HECUBA *joins her, left.*

CICELY *(after a moment)* It happened last week...as I was leaving the office.

She stops as though wondering if to continue.

HECUBA *(prompting)* Yes?

CICELY There was a man. Outside the estate agents. *(quickly)* I knew I'd seen him before, but couldn't think where. I was halfway down the street before it came to me. It was Quentin Danesworth. That dreadful little man from Channel Five. "What on earth's he doing here?" I thought. So instead of driving off, I waited till he came out and went back to have a word with Mavis. *(confidentially)* We've a little arrangement, so I knew there wouldn't be a problem. *(hurrying on)* Well to cut a long story short, he was asking about this place. Who the present owners were, and might they be interested in selling? *(quickly)* Of course, she knew nothing so you needn't worry about her. But he did say something strange before he left.

HECUBA Strange?

CICELY *(quoting)* "By the time I've finished, the public'll be swarming round it like flies." *(concerned)* I couldn't think what he meant, or what had brought him to this part of the world, but if he'd got his eye on Monument House, it could only spell trouble. He's ruined more lives than the parson preached about. Getting his foot in the door could expose you all. *(earnestly)* I worried about it for days, and though Vesta insisted I never came here again, I just had to warn you. In case he turned up here.

HECUBA *(balefully)* He already has, dear. Along with other unwanted visitors. *(reassuringly)* But you needn't have worried. None of them will be leaving. It's all under control.

CICELY *(with a relieved sigh)* I should have known. *(admiringly)* No one steals a march on Hecuba. *(brightly)* Well...it looks like I've wasted my time, then. But I couldn't take the chance of you being off guard if the Danesworth man did arrive here. We've always had the family's interests at heart, as well you know. *(correcting herself)* Well...Father and I have. The less said about Crayle and Penworthy, the better. *(regretfully)* If only I'd suspected... *(pulling herself together and rising)* Still...it's water under the bridge. The main thing is, you won't be caught out.

HECUBA *(surprised)* You're not going?

She rises.

CICELY *(regretfully)* It's pretty thick tonight and I don't want to take any chances.

HECUBA *(fussily)* Then why don't you stay? There's plenty of room and I'm sure the children will be only too pleased to meet you when I tell them how considerate you've been.

CICELY *(reluctantly)* I'd better not. *(moving behind the settee)* Let's see how they react when they know I dropped in. Where are they, by the way?

HECUBA Drusilla's settling the visitors, and Posti's—

SIR BEVERLEY *(offstage left; calling)* Strickland? Strickland? What are you doing up there? Having a bloody bath?

CICELY gives HECUBA a questioning look.

HECUBA *(tight-lipped)* One of our "visitors". A most unpleasant man. I can't wait to see the back of him.

SIR BEVERLEY *(offstage; calling)* Strickland.

HECUBA *(glowering)* All that bellowing. Obviously not a gentleman.

ANTHONY *(offstage; calling breathlessly)* Sorry, Sir. I was trying the other one.

SIR BEVERLEY *(offstage; calling)* Never mind the excuses. Did you get him, for me?

ANTHONY *(offstage)* No signal, Sir. It really is a dead spot.

SIR BEVERLEY *(offstage; scathingly)* Bloody provinces. If it's not fog, it's communications. Send him an e-mail, then. And get your finger out.

ANTHONY *(offstage)* I'll do it now, Sir

CICELY *(drily)* I see what you mean. If that man was my boss, I'd poison him myself.

HECUBA *(primly)* He certainly won't be missed, I can assure you. *(fussily)* Now you're sure you'd rather not stay? It wouldn't be a problem. You could help us dispose of the bodies in the morning.

CICELY *(sweetly)* You're very kind, Hecuba, but I really must get back. I've a meeting first thing tomorrow and it's more than my reputation's worth to be late for it. *(seeing the dish)* Oh. Turkish Delight. Can I steal a piece for the journey?

She goes to take one.

HECUBA *(hastily)* Not those, dear. I've rolled them in antimony for the guests. Don't want you dying of liver failure, do we?

She chuckles.

CICELY *(pulling her hand back hastily)* No. I – er – don't think we do. *(smiling weakly and moving towards the door)* I'll see myself out, shall I?

HECUBA *(firmly)* You'll do no such thing. The least I can do is escort my friends to the door. *(primly)* It may be fashionable to sneer at courtesy these days, but as long as I'm mistress of Monument House, simple good manners stay paramount.

DRUSILLA *enters, stops short and stares at* **CICELY**.

(guiltily) Drusilla, my dear. You don't know Miss Venner, do you?

CICELY *(extending her hand)* I wondered when I was going to meet you.

She smiles.

DRUSILLA *(ignoring her)* Get her out of here. *(sharply)* Now.

HECUBA *(offended)* I will not have rudeness in this house, Drusilla. Poor Cicely's...

CICELY *(hastily)* Look. I didn't want to intrude...

DRUSILLA *(snapping)* Then you shouldn't have come here, should you? Gran told you to keep away. She didn't want you near Monument House. In her opinion, you shared responsibility for everything that happened here.

HECUBA *(staunchly)* Which was quite unfair. Cicely had nothing to do with Crayle and Penworthy.

DRUSILLA *(harshly)* So you keep telling us...but it doesn't bring the others back, does it?

CICELY If you'd let me explain...

DRUSILLA I don't want your explanations. I just want you out of here.

CICELY *(conceding; to* HECUBA*)* I'll speak to you later.

SIR BEVERLEY *appears in the doorway.*

SIR BEVERLEY *(sourly)* Does anything work in this place? *(entering)* I've been trying to contact my office for the past half hour and - *(seeing* CICELY *and reacting)* Bloody Hell's Bells. What are you doing here?

CICELY *(startled)* Sir Beverley.

DRUSILLA *and* HECUBA *look surprised.*

SIR BEVERLEY *(moving to her, hand extended)* Must be five years. How are you?

They shake hands.

Not here on business, are you?

CICELY *(hastily)* No, no. Just visiting Hecuba – Mrs Tomb. But what are you—

SIR BEVERLEY *(bluffing)* Oh, taking a few days off, that's all. Recharging batteries, and all that. Health farm sounded just the job, so I thought I'd give this place a try. *(changing the subject)* So. Where've you been keeping yourself? We've not heard a word since you left the firm. Thought you really had buggered off to foreign climes and forgotten all about us.

CICELY *(forcing a smile)* Not much chance of that, Sir Beverley. It'd be hard to forget you. No. I came back here when Father died. To help run the partnership. We've an office in Burnham. Not too big, but with a good reputation.

HECUBA *(proudly)* They've looked after our family since Georgian times.

DRUSILLA *glares at her and moves down right.*

SIR BEVERLEY *(to CICELY; curiously)* You're not part of this set-up, are you?

CICELY *(puzzled)* Set-up?

SIR BEVERLEY *(pointedly)* The Tomb family business.

CICELY *(amused)* Good heavens, no. What I know about antiques could be written on the back of a postage stamp. It's conveyancing and run-of-the-mill these days. Not much call for corporate in this neck of the woods. *(gushingly)* It's been lovely seeing you again, Sir Beverley. Especially after all this time. But I really must dash. *(playfully)* Perhaps we could meet up tomorrow? A drink at the Regent Hotel?

SIR BEVERLEY Sounds perfect. I'll make a reservation, shall I? Twelve thirty-ish?

CICELY I'll be there on the dot.

CICELY *gives them all a quick smile and exits rapidly.*

SIR BEVERLEY *(to the others)* So you know Cissie Bonnington, eh? Now there's a turn-up for the books.

DRUSILLA *(raising an eyebrow)* Bonnington?

She glances at HECUBA.

SIR BEVERLEY *(moving round to sit on the settee)* Best legal secretary ever worked for me. Despite the false modesty. She's a mind like a razor, that one.

DRUSILLA *(acidly)* I'm sure. But she calls herself Venner these days.

SIR BEVERLEY Probably her maiden name. Not surprising after what went on. They'd have tarred her with the same brush if she hadn't done a bunk and vanished.

DRUSILLA *and* HECUBA *look puzzled.*

Husband swindled a fortune from the firm he worked for, then scarpered when the police came round and started digging. Never found him, of course, but they recovered some of the cash, though most of it's still missing. Popular theory had it she were involved as well, but I couldn't see it myself. There were no evidence, and she'd an alibi like concrete. I were out in Zambia when she left us, and often wondered where she'd gone. *(back to business)* But never mind that. What's going on with my problem? You told me an hour, two hours ago, and I'm still not hearing owt. Is summat being done, or isn't it?

DRUSILLA *(smoothly)* It's all been taken care of, Sir Beverley. By tomorrow, your worries will be over.

SIR BEVERLEY *(relieved)* And about bloody time. But if this happens again, I'll expect some sort of discount for inconvenience. I've more to do with my hours than waste 'em by chasing up defaulters. *(changing the subject)* Is there any chance of a cuppa in this place? My throat's like sandpaper.

DRUSILLA *(glowering)* I'm sure we can find something to suit your taste. *(to* HECUBA*)* Aunt Hecuba?

HECUBA *(giving an evil smile)* I'll see what I can do.

HECUBA *makes for the door and exits.*

SIR BEVERLEY *(calling after her)* And tell Strickland I want him in here. *(muttering)* Though why I landed myself with him, I've no idea. He's as much use as a rubber tin-opener. Can't even use a bloody mobile.

DRUSILLA *(mildly)* Hardly his fault, Sir Beverley. The signals almost non-existent here, and even the landline's been out for days. I'm sure he does his best.

SIR BEVERLEY *(drily)* He'd not last a day with Alan Sugar. So why should I have to suffer?

CICELY *enters.*

CICELY *(apologetically)* Sorry to be a nuisance, but it's my front tyre. I must have run over a nail, or something. It's absolutely flat.

SIR BEVERLEY *(rising)* I'll have Strickland change it for you.

CICELY *(worried)* But that's it. I haven't a spare. I've not picked it up from the last time.

SIR BEVERLEY *(shrugging)* He can give you a lift, then.

CICELY *(relieved)* Would you mind? I'd be so grateful. I really do have to get back.

ANTHONY *appears in the doorway.*

ANTHONY You wanted me, Sir Beverley?

SIR BEVERLEY Lady's got a puncture and no spare. Run her back to Burnham and make it quick.

ANTHONY *(dismayed)* In this?

SIR BEVERLEY Bit of fog won't hurt you. Just don't scratch the bloody paintwork. And what's happened with the e-mail?

ANTHONY *(helplessly)* I can't seem to send it, sir. There must be something wrong.

SIR BEVERLEY *(gritting his teeth)* For crying out loud. Is there anything you can do? *(testily)* Never mind. Just take her to Burnham and make sure she gets there in one piece.

ANTHONY *(flustered)* Yes, Sir Beverley.

He looks at CICELY *helplessly and she crosses him to exit. He follows her unhappily.*

SIR BEVERLEY *(sourly)* You couldn't dispose of him by way of compensation, could you? God knows what they're teaching 'em at university these days. It's certainly not common sense. *(sitting again)* So what's the deal with Logan, then? How are you going to do it?

DRUSILLA *(smoothly)* That's something you don't need to know, Sir Beverley. Just take my word, it's all in hand.

HECUBA *enters with a tray. On it, a china cup and saucer, spoon, milk jug and sugar bowl. She moves round to* SIR BEVERLEY.

HECUBA *(beaming)* One cup of tea.

She extends the tray to him.

SIR BEVERLEY *(peering into the cup, suspiciously)* Not a tea bag job, is it?

HECUBA *(shocked)* Certainly not. It's our own special blend. Once you've tasted it, you'll never drink anything else. *(sweetly)* Milk and sugar?

SIR BEVERLEY Never touch the stuff. And what's the poncey smell?

HECUBA Cinnamon and lemon salts.

SIR BEVERLEY *(dismissing it)* I'm not into fancy concoctions. Earl-bloody-Greys and Orange-flamin'-Pekoe. Haven't you any Typhoo?

HECUBA *(frustrated)* But I particularly made this for you.

The internal telephone rings.

DRUSILLA I'll get it. *(crossing to the phone and picking it up)* Reception.

HECUBA *(to* SIR BEVERLEY*)* You could at least try it.

SIR BEVERLEY *(scowling)* What part of "no"'s evading you? If you haven't got real tea, I'll have coffee. And make sure it's hot.

DRUSILLA *replaces the phone as a tight-lipped* HECUBA *makes for the door with the tray.*

DRUSILLA *(stopping* HECUBA*)* Could you take a hot-water bottle to Mr Danesworth's room, Heckie. He's feeling a little chilled. I'll attend to Sir Beverley.

HECUBA *scowls, hands* DRUCILLA *the tray and exits huffily.*

(lightly) We don't appear to be doing well with our social graces, do we? Perhaps a health farm wasn't such a good idea?

SIR BEVERLEY *(gruffly)* Stick to the business you do know, my motto.

ANTHONY *enters, looking concerned.*

What is it now?

ANTHONY It's your car, Sir Beverley. The tyres are flat on that. Front and back.

SIR BEVERLEY *(surprised)* What?

ANTHONY *(worried)* It looks like someone's slashed them.

SIR BEVERLEY *(annoyed and rising)* Is this a bloody joke?

ANTHONY *(helplessly)* You can see for yourself.

SIR BEVERLEY *storms out.*

ANTHONY *and* DRUSILLA *look at each other in bewilderment.*

DRUSILLA *puts the tray on the table behind the settee and exits with* ANTHONY.

PHILLIPA *(offstage; calling)* Excuse me. *(trying again)* Miss Tomb...

DAPHNE *(offstage; calling)* Miss Tomb.

PHILLIPA *(offstage)* Oh, do feel free to ignore me.

PHILLIPA *appears in the doorway.* DAPHNE *appears behind her.*

DAPHNE They seemed in an awful hurry, Phillipa. We're not on fire, are we?

PHILLIPA *(entering the room)* If we are, I'm staying right where I am. It's like the inside of a freezer. What's happened to the heating? It was fine during dinner.

She crosses to the fireplace and holds out her hands to the fire.

DAPHNE *(entering)* I don't feel it so much, myself. Perhaps the boiler's gone out? *(helpfully)* I could get you a wrap.

PHILLIPA It's not worth the bother. Half nine or not, I'm heading upstairs as soon as I've had a drink. At least I'll be warm under the covers.

DAPHNE *(spotting the tray)* There's a cup of something here. *(touching it)* And it's still hot. Tea, I think.

PHILLIPA I'll settle for a gin, if you don't mind. They'll not miss a drop of that. *(heading for the drinks table)* Fancy one yourself?

DAPHNE *(reproachfully)* You know I don't, Phillipa. I never touch alcohol. *(wistfully)* I wouldn't mind a cup of tea, though.

PHILLIPA *(pouring herself a gin)* Help yourself to that one. It's probably Mrs T's, but it'll be cold by the time she puts in an

appearance. *(glancing round)* I thought she was supposed
to be cleaning this place?

DAPHNE *(reluctantly)* I'd better not. It wouldn't seem right.

PHILLIPA Suit yourself.

She prepares to drink.

DAPHNE *(eyeing the tea)* It does seem a waste, though.

PHILLIPA *(sighing)* Then drink it. At least one of you'll have
the benefit. She can always make another.

DAPHNE *picks up the cup and saucer, hesitates, then
puts milk into the cup and stirs.*

(suddenly) What was that?

DAPHNE What?

PHILLIPA *(frowning)* That scraping noise.

She puts the glass down.

DAPHNE *(puzzled)* I didn't hear anything.

PHILLIPA *(looking at the secret panel)* It came from over there.

DAPHNE *(looking at it askance)* Are you sure?

PHILLIPA Not entirely, but...

MIRANDA *enters from the hall.*

MIRANDA *(in her "little girl" voice again)* Sorry to bother you,
but I'm looking for Bobby – my husband. He seems to have
vanished. *(helplessly)* I can't find him anywhere.

DAPHNE *(excitedly)* Oh, Phillipa. It's just like your book.
"Whatever happened to Henry?"

PHILLIPA *(wincing)* Don't be melodramatic, Daffs. She's not
likely to find him bricked up behind a wall, is she?

DAPHNE *looks abashed and moves to sit on the settee,
taking her tea with her.*

Perhaps he's gone for a stroll? Though I can't see him walking round the grounds in this lot. The fog's bad enough, but the smell...

MIRANDA *(clutching her throat theatrically)* I know. I thought I was losing my voice.

DAPHNE *sips at her tea, grimaces and recoils from it. Reaching over the settee back, she replaces it on the tray.*

PHILLIPA Have you asked the Tombs if they've seen him?

MIRANDA I can't find them, either. I'm so worried.

DAPHNE *(suddenly)* You don't think...

She stops.

PHILLIPA What?

DAPHNE *(reluctantly)* Well...he might have gone back in there? *(looking at the panel)* For another look round. And got lost.

MIRANDA *(breathlessly)* Oh, no. He doesn't like dark places. Not at all.

DAPHNE But we did hear a noise a few minutes ago, didn't we, Phillipa?

PHILLIPA I did, you mean. Though I could have imagined it. And besides...how would he get in there? Mr Danesworth's the only one who knows how to open it.

MIRANDA *(brightly)* Oh, no. I can do it, too. I found it by accident.

DAPHNE *turns to watch as she goes to the panel and runs her fingers over the woodwork.*

It's here.

She presses.

The panel opens to reveal QUENTIN *standing there, his throat cut from ear to ear, his front covered with blood.*

MIRANDA *and* PHILLIPA *react with shock.* DAPHNE *is motionless, her attention seemingly fixed on* QUENTIN, *who crumples to the floor.*

PHILLIPA *(gaping at him)* Oh, my God. Don't look Daffy. Don't look.

DAPHNE *remains motionless.*

(noticing) Daffy? *(more urgently)* Daffy? *(hurrying over to her)* I told you not to look.

She touches DAPHNE*'s shoulder.*

DAPHNE *topples sideways onto the settee, dead. The two women stare in horror.*

Lights fade.

Curtain.

ACT II

Scene One

The same. Half an hour later.

The secret panel is closed, but otherwise the room is unchanged. DRUSILLA *is hunched in the wing chair, her back to the others, seemingly mopping her eyes with a crumpled handkerchief.* HECUBA *stands just behind her, hand resting on* DRUSILLA's *left shoulder.* CICELY *sits on the settee arm right, a glass of brandy in her hand and her handbag by her feet,* MIRANDA *is on the settee with* ROBERT *beside her, arm protectively around her.* SIR BEVERLEY *stands by the table left, and* ANTHONY *sits on the pulled-out desk chair, facing into the room. All appear shocked.*

SIR BEVERLEY *(grimly)* I don't see we have much choice. Like it, or not, we've got to get the police here.

CICELY *(nodding)* I quite agree, Sir Beverley. But how? As Hecuba's told us, the landline's out of commission, and mobiles don't operate in this area. *(helpfully)* The only way we can make contact right now, is for someone to walk to Haslow and make a call from there.

She sips at her drink.

SIR BEVERLEY In that case, we'll need a volunteer. *(looking at* ANTHONY*)* Strickland.

ANTHONY *(looking up; startled)* Yes, Sir?

SIR BEVERLEY You'll be wanting a torch.

ANTHONY *looks at him blankly.*

(acidly) Knowing your sense of direction, you'd probably end up in the river.

ANTHONY *looks dismayed.*

ROBERT *(frowning)* Couldn't it wait till morning? It might have cleared by then.

MIRANDA *(in her "little girl" voice)* Bobby's right. We don't want another accident, do we?

SIR BEVERLEY *(sarcastically)* I'd hardly call slitting your throat an accident, Miss Torrence. In my opinion, he knew exactly what he was doing, and made a damned good job of it.

ROBERT *(protesting)* But why commit suicide here?

SIR BEVERLEY *(drily)* I shouldn't think that's too much of a mystery. *(moving behind the settee)* I hear a lot in my line of work, and the word is that ratings for his show were dropping faster than a politician's trousers. His backers were pulling out at the end of the month.

MIRANDA *(bewildered)* But finding this place would have put him at the top again. He told me so.

HECUBA *(firmly)* Not without our permission. Monument House is a family home, and the last thing we need here are strangers tramping around it, poking their cameras into things that don't concern them.

CICELY *(gently)* Hecuba's right, Miss Torrence. The poor man must have been desperate. When he realized his programme would never materialize, he decided to kill himself on the site of his greatest discovery.

There is a short silence.

ANTHONY *(puzzled)* But why in there? *(indicating the panel)* Why not in his room?

SIR BEVERLEY *(bluntly)* Because he never intended being found. The Tombs had no idea that passage even existed till he arrived. They hadn't a clue how he opened it, decided it looked dangerous when they did see it, and closed it up again without asking too many questions. He'd be pretty confident they'd not go looking in there for him. They'd think he'd done a bunk without paying, and be only too pleased to see the back of him. *(glancing down at* **MIRANDA***)* And if it hadn't been for her, he'd have vanished forever and the Summers woman would still've been with us.

ROBERT *(hotly)* You're not blaming Miranda...

CICELY *(soothingly)* Of course not. What Sir Beverley means is that nobody knew Miss Summers had a bad heart. Not even her friend. And the shock of seeing him with his throat cut...well...

She breaks off.

There is a short silence as they dwell on the thought. **SIR BEVERLEY** *suddenly focuses on* **ROBERT** *and frowns.*

ANTHONY *(puzzled)* But who disabled the cars? *(helplessly)* Tyres slashed. Fuel tanks drained. Leads ripped out. And why?

SIR BEVERLEY *(still looking at* **ROBERT***)* Danesworth, of course. As the Tombs had ruined his life, he wanted to make damned sure they'd get it in the neck from us for the damage he'd caused. *(moving left again; looking puzzled)* Vindictive little swine.

ROBERT *(reluctantly)* I suppose it does make sense. *(remembering)* But what about his own car? I mean... Where is it? Ours are out there. But what's happened to his?

ANTHONY *(frowning)* That's right. He couldn't have got here without one.

He rises.

SIR BEVERLEY *(dismissively)* Probably came by taxi.

ROBERT Then how was he supposed to leave again? If the phone doesn't work, he obviously couldn't call.

SIR BEVERLEY *(patiently)* But he wouldn't have known that then, would he? And who's to say he wouldn't have walked? *(sourly)* Or minced.

ROBERT Not with a suitcase as big as his. It's twice the size of mine.

SIR BEVERLEY *(frowning)* And how would you know?

ROBERT Because I've seen it. In his room.

HECUBA *(sharply)* What were you doing in there? You'd no right.

ROBERT *(taken aback)* I don't see it's any of your business, but I wanted to talk to him about an offer he'd made to Miranda.

MIRANDA *(helpfully)* He'd asked me to guest on his next show.

SIR BEVERLEY *(acidly)* What next show? By the end of the month, he wouldn't have had a job, never mind a bloody show.

CICELY *(ignoring this)* And what did he say to you?

ROBERT *(still irritated)* He didn't say anything. He wasn't there.

SIR BEVERLEY *(brusquely)* Well, this is getting us nowhere. What we do need to do is get Strickland off to Haslow, and the police here to sort things out. God knows how long we're going to be penned up.

ROBERT *looks at him questioningly.*

CICELY *(explaining)* Till everything's sorted out. They'll be wanting statements, etc., so I expect it'll be a few days, at least.

She sips at her drink.

ROBERT *(dismayed)* Days? But we can't stay in this place. We're on our honeymoon. We've rooms booked all over the place.

SIR BEVERLEY *(acidly)* And I'm sure the rest of us have better things to do than twiddle us thumbs while they're prodding and poking about in innocent people's lives. But like I said earlier, we don't have much choice. We've two dead bodies

on the premises and something's got to be done about 'em.
(to ANTHONY*)* You can call a garage while you're at it and
see about getting the cars fixed. Then give Dobson a call
and tell him where we are. I'll deal with the Logan bid as
soon as we're back.

He begins to cough.

ANTHONY *nods.*

(impatiently) Well, go on, then.

He gets his inhaler out and doses himself.

ANTHONY *(smiling wanly)* I'll get my coat.

ANTHONY *exits reluctantly.*

ROBERT *(calling after him)* And watch where you're going.

MIRANDA *(suddenly)* Ohhhhhh.

All but DRUSILLA *quickly look at* MIRANDA.

ROBERT *(anxiously)* What is it?

MIRANDA *(faintly)* I don't feel well.

CICELY *(rising)* Probably delayed shock. You'd better lie down.

MIRANDA *(weakly)* Oh, yes. Yes.

ROBERT *(anxiously)* Let me help you.

He rises rapidly and helps her to her feet.

MIRANDA *(theatrically)* Ohhhh. *(She slumps in his arms)*

ROBERT *(supporting her)* It's all right, darling. You're going
to be fine.

CICELY I'll give you a hand with her.

*She collects her handbag, puts her glass down and helps
support* MIRANDA.

MIRANDA, ROBERT *and* CICELY *move to the door and
exit.*

The moment they've gone, **SIR BEVERLEY** *replaces his inhaler, moves to the door and closes it, before turning to face the others.*

SIR BEVERLEY *(harshly)* Right. You can switch off the crocodile tears. If we don't work fast, we're all in trouble.

DRUSILLA *(turning to face him; all trace of distress gone)* Trouble?

SIR BEVERLEY I mightn't be Hercule Poirot, but even I know he didn't slit his own throat. You don't need hot water bottles if you're planning to end it all. *(sneering)* If this is a sample of what you've got on offer these days, then the deal's off. I thought you lot were infallible. That little effort was a cock-up from beginning to end.

DRUSILLA *(rising; icily)* I quite agree, Sir Beverley. But Danesworth's death had nothing to do with us. Somebody beat us to it.

HECUBA *(huffily)* And besides...he was killed with a knife. *(primly)* None of the Tombs would use a knife. It's far too common...

SIR BEVERLEY *(scornfully)* And what about the other one? Who killed her? The bloody Tooth Fairy? *(amused)* You don't expect the police to believe it was a heart attack, do you? *(shaking his head)* They've only to look at her eyes to see what finished her off. Pupils were like pinpoints. *(harshly)* She were poisoned.

DRUSILLA *looks at* **HECUBA**, *suspiciously.*

So what did you have against her, then? *(suddenly)* Or was it a mistake? Perhaps you got the wrong victim?

HECUBA *(bridling)* I beg your pardon?

SIR BEVERLEY *(pointedly)* I notice the tea you made me's still here. *(indicating it with his head)* And somebody's put milk in it. Summat I never touch. *(musing)* I wonder if she drank some of that?

HECUBA *(affronted)* There was nothing wrong with that tea, Sir Beverley. Nothing at all. People have drunk it for years without complaining.

SIR BEVERLEY *(drily)* P'raps they never got the chance?

HECUBA *(glaring at him, crossing to the tray, picking up the cup, drinking the contents, replacing the cup and looking at him defiantly)* Does that satisfy you?

SIR BEVERLEY *(after a pause)* Well...maybe I was wrong about the tea...but she were poisoned. I know that as sure as I know my own name, and the plods'll pick it up a damn sight faster than I did, believe you me...

HECUBA *(still seething)* Which clearly proves it had nothing to do with us. If we had been involved, not a soul would have known about it. *(proudly)* Our poisons are family secrets and completely untraceable.

DRUSILLA *(moving down right; puzzled)* But if it wasn't us who killed them. It has to be one of the others. And why immobilize the cars? It doesn't make sense. Unless... *(suddenly realizing and turning to face them)* The Venner woman.

SIR BEVERLEY *(frowning)* What about her?

DRUSILLA *(icily)* I don't know how well you really know her, but she's not been welcome in Monument House since Gran inherited the place. Till the day she died, she suspected Penworthy, Venner and Crayle had something to do with the family's misfortunes.

HECUBA *(indignantly)* And quite without reason in my opinion. Cicely's been nothing but supportive to the family since the day we met.

SIR BEVERLEY *(surprised)* You mean she knows what you do for a living?

HECUBA *(backtracking)* Of course not. She doesn't suspect a thing. But it's ridiculous to think that all the partners were involved in what happened here. *(defensively)* If I thought otherwise, I'd have killed her myself. And besides...even if she was involved, why come out here to kill strangers? It's us she'd be trying to get rid of.

DRUSILLA *(acidly)* And what makes you think that she isn't? Last year's inquiry almost finished the business. If Monica's body had turned up, they'd still be rooting round here.

HECUBA *(hotly)* And who suggested Monica could have killed them all before leaving the country with the family fortune? *(pointedly)* Cicely Venner. If it hadn't been for her, who knows what verdict they'd have brought in? *(bitterly)* The way your grandmother treated her was shameful.

DRUSILLA *(tightly)* It's neither time or place to start that again, Aunt Heckie, but I do know this much. If the police find more bodies in Monument House, we can say goodbye to all the plans we've been making so busily.

HECUBA *(huffily)* Which I was never consulted about. As usual. And as for the police—

DRUSILLA *(cutting in sharply)* Well, I'm sure Sir Beverley's thought of a workable solution to that problem.

She looks at him questioningly.

SIR BEVERLEY *(smugly)* As a matter of fact, I have. And you two are in the perfect position to make sure they never get wind of what's happened here.

DRUSILLA *(frowning)* But you've sent Strickland to call them.

SIR BEVERLEY *(sourly)* That was for everyone else's benefit. *(bluffly)* But it's a long walk to Haslow, and who's to say he'll get there safely in fog like this? If he missed his way, for instance, and fell into this marsh you mentioned earlier?

HECUBA *(surprised)* You mean we should dispose of him?

DRUSILLA *(cutting in)* Exactly my own thought, Sir Beverley. I just wasn't sure you'd agree.

SIR BEVERLEY Why not? The man's a liability. He was up for the chop the minute we got back to London, so I'm hardly likely to miss him. He's the worst PA I've ever had. No use to man or beast.

DRUSILLA *(briskly)* Then we'll deal with him first.

SIR BEVERLEY *(flatly)* You'll have to get your skates on. He'll be halfway down the drive by now. Providing he's managed to find it.

DRUSILLA *(confidently)* Don't worry. He'll never make it to Haslow.

SIR BEVERLEY *(sardonically)* And how're you going to stop him?

DRUSILLA *(smiling coldly)* We have our ways.

She gets out her mobile phone and begins punching out a number.

SIR BEVERLEY *(frowning)* I thought there weren't any signals from here.

DRUSILLA *(concentrating on her task)* There aren't. Unless we want one. Gran installed a blocker the day we moved in. Without the right code, you can't get a signal for at least half a mile. *(into the phone)* Posti? Where are you now? ...Good. Now listen. We need your assistance. *(looking at* SIR BEVERLEY*)* Sir Beverley's PA is heading for Haslow to call the police. He has to vanish before he gets there. Can you arrange that? ...Of course not. It was Sir Beverley's suggestion. He's no further use for him... Exactly. Then we'll leave it to you. *(ending the call and smiling)* Problem solved.

SIR BEVERLEY And what about the others? You can't risk them leaving, either.

DRUSILLA The honeymooners are in the turret room, so the bed will take care of them...

HECUBA *(explaining)* It's a four-poster. Cousin Caligula built it himself. *(beaming)* Such a wonderful craftsman. Half an hour after the bedside lights go off, the canopy comes down and suffocates the sleeper. *(regretfully)* It was a pity he forgot to tell his wife he'd finished it. *(brightly)* But she had a lovely funeral,

DRUSILLA *(rolling her eyes)* And Heckie and I will deal with the rest.

SIR BEVERLEY Good. Then I think I'll call it a night. There's a couple of things need my attention before I drop off, and I hate going to bed with a mind full of questions. *(nodding at* DRUSILLA's *mobile)* I'll borrow that, if you don't mind?

He extends his hand for it.

DRUSILLA I don't think so, Sir Beverley. The fewer who know your whereabouts, the less chance of mistakes.

She puts the phone away.

SIR BEVERLEY *(acidly)* When I need lessons in egg-sucking, young lady, I'll not be requiring 'em from somebody barely out of nappies.

DRUSILLA *stares at him defiantly.*

(fuming) All right. Have it your own way. If it's not too much trouble, you can send me up a decent cup of tea and I'll see you in the morning.

SIR BEVERLEY *exits, leaving the door open behind him.*

HECUBA *(seething)* How dare he speak to us like that?

DRUSILLA *(mildly)* Will you finish him off, or shall I?

HECUBA *(surprised)* You mean I can try again? You wouldn't mind?

DRUSILLA Why should I? We're family, aren't we?

HECUBA *(beaming)* Oh, Drusilla. That's the nicest thing you've ever said to me.

DRUSILLA *(frowning)* There is one thing, though. The tea you drank.

HECUBA *(remembering)* It was perfectly safe. There was nothing in the cup. The poison was on the saucer. It was one of Athene's favourite methods. That's why I wanted him to have it. It would have been so appropriate after all the nasty things he said about her. The minute the Summers woman lifted it, she absorbed it through her fingers and that was the end of her.

She smirks.

DRUSILLA So what have you in mind for Sir Beverley?

HECUBA *(thoughtfully)* I looked through the records before dinner. His grandfather was a ship's captain, according to Septimus Tomb, and most of their money came from seafaring. *(deciding)* So Captain Bligh should do the trick. *(primly)* One of my own specialities. And most unpleasant, I can promise you. I'll prepare it at once.

Hugging herself with excitement, she exits.

DRUSILLA *watches her go, then sinks into deep thought and drifts towards the French windows to gaze blankly into the gardens. After a moment, she comes to a decision and turns to exit.*

PHILLIPA *enters, looking wan.*

DRUSILLA *(surprised)* Miss Collins.

PHILLIPA *(brokenly)* I've been sitting with her. In her bedroom. *(moving to the settee)* Wondering what to do. I'd no idea she had a heart problem. She never mentioned it. *(sitting on the settee)* Do you think they'll be long?

DRUSILLA *(puzzled)* Who?

PHILLIPA The police. Miss Venner said someone had gone for them.

DRUSILLA Oh...yes. Mr Strickland. Sir Beverley's PA. He left a few minutes ago. *(shrugging)* It depends how quickly he can walk in fog like this.

PHILLIPA *(slightly alarmed)* But how do you know he didn't do it?

DRUSILLA *(blankly)* Do what?

PHILLIPA *(insistently)* Kill Mr Danesworth.

DRUSILLA *(pretending incomprehension)* No one killed Mr Danesworth. He committed suicide.

PHILLIPA *(shaking her head)* No, no. He didn't. He was left-handed.

DRUSILLA *(puzzled)* I'm sorry?

PHILLIPA *(firmly)* Quentin Danesworth was left-handed...but his throat was cut from left to right. I saw it at once. It's the same mistake my murderer makes in *Too Many Graves*.

DRUSILLA *(shaken)* I'm sure you're mistaken.

PHILLIPA *(shaking her head)* Someone cut his throat from behind, then hid him in the secret passage.

DRUSILLA *(pretending disbelief)* But that's ridiculous. Who'd want to kill an absolute stranger? And why do it here?

PHILLIPA I've no idea. But it must have been a spur-of-the-moment thing, because whoever killed him wouldn't dare have risked being close when the body was found. Not being trapped in the house, as we are.

DRUSILLA *(pretending amusement)* Hardly trapped, Miss Collins. No one's a prisoner here. I know the vehicles have been vandalized, but Haslow's only a few miles down the road, and we've all got legs.

PHILLIPA *(ignoring this)* Finding that passage was a godsend. After what your aunt said about the danger of exploring it without knowing what condition it was in, it might never have been opened up again. It became the perfect place to hide the body. And if it hadn't been for Miss Torrence, the killer could have got away with it. Now it's just a matter of time.

DRUSILLA *(pretending shock)* But this is our house. We can't have a murder here. You must be mistaken.

She turns away right.

PHILLIPA *(rising,)* I'm sorry. I didn't mean to blurt it out like that. *(moving closer to* DRUSILLA*)* But whoever's responsible killed Daffy as well...albeit without knowing...and I can't let them get away with that.

A breathless ANTHONY *hurries into the room, wearing his topcoat.*

ANTHONY *(gasping)* Miss Tomb. Miss Tomb.

DRUSILLA *(turning to him; surprised)* Mr Strickland.

PHILLIPA *turns to see him.*

ANTHONY *(gasping)* Outside. There's a man. At least I think it's a man. I couldn't really tell. But he's carrying a gun.

PHILLIPA *looks startled.*

DRUSILLA *(blankly)* Who is he?

ANTHONY *(helplessly)* I've no idea. But I spotted him at the bend in the drive. The fog cleared for a second and there he was. Moving towards the house with a gun in his hand. Like Clint Eastwood in *Dirty Harry*.

PHILLIPA Are you sure you weren't seeing things?

ANTHONY *(incredulously)* You don't mistake things that size. It looked like a cannon. *(anxiously)* Where's Sir Beverley?

DRUSILLA *(baffled)* In his room, I expect. But...

ANTHONY *(hastily)* I've got to warn him. It could be him that's in danger. He's always talking about industrial espionage, and someone could have followed us from London.

PHILLIPA But not to shoot him? Surely?

ANTHONY *(helplessly)* You never know in this day and age. Some people will do anything.

ANTHONY *hurries out again.*

ROBERT *(offstage)* Something wrong?

ANTHONY *(offstage)* I'll explain later.

ROBERT *and* CICELY *enter the room*

CICELY *(to* DRUSILLA*)* She's fast asleep. Definitely the shock. *(moving to the settee)* I'm feeling quite wobbly myself.

She sits.

ROBERT *(moving behind the settee to centre)* And I'd not say no to a drink, if there's anything on offer?

DRUSILLA Of course. *(to* CICELY*; coldly)* Miss Venner?

CICELY *shakes her head.*

(to PHILLIPA*)* Miss Collins?

PHILLIPA *shakes her head.*

(to ROBERT*)* Will whisky be all right?

ROBERT Fine.

DRUSILLA *(indicating the drinks table)* Then please help yourself. I must have a word with Aunt Hecuba.

Before DRUSILLA *can move,* HECUBA *enters with a small tray which holds a cup of tea, and moves behind the settee.*

HECUBA *(happily)* Captain Bligh. *(Realizing the others are there)* Oh.

PHILLIPA Bligh???

HECUBA *(hastily)* He was played by Charles Laughton. *(explaining)* A famous actor, in his day. Died in the nineteen sixties *(still improvising)* Sir Beverley asked me about him, and I just remembered on my way to his room. Such a talented man. And almost a double for Septimus Tomb. Wouldn't you say, Drusilla?

DRUSILLA I wouldn't know. I'm too young.

ANTHONY *stumbles into the room, looking stunned and shocked.*

ANTHONY Sir Beverley. I think he's dead.

All react.

HECUBA *(protesting)* But he can't be. He's not touched his tea yet.

She displays the tray.

ANTHONY *(weakly)* He's slumped in the chair like some awful rag doll.

DRUSILLA *(puzzled)* But he was fine a few minutes ago.

HECUBA *(put out)* And I made this specially for him. Who's going to drink it now? *(glowering)* Some people have no consideration.

ANTHONY *(suddenly)* What shall I say at the office?

He stumbles to the right side of the settee.

ROBERT *(concerned)* Are you sure he's dead? Do you want me to look at him?

All regard him.

(explaining) I did first aid with the St John's Ambulance.

ANTHONY *(dully; sitting next to* **CICELY***)* It must have been his asthma. His inhaler's on the floor beside him.

DRUSILLA *(warily)* You didn't—?

ANTHONY *(hastily)* Oh, no. No. I'd never seen a body before I came here, so the idea of touching one...

He shudders and looks down.

CICELY *pats his hand in a comforting manner.*

PHILLIPA *(practically)* Well, before we all start throwing wobblies, it'd be a good idea to see if he actually is dead. He could be just unconscious.

CICELY Exactly my own thought. Though it wouldn't surprise me if asthma had finished him off. He'd some pretty bad attacks in the time I was at Comstock Enterprises.

DRUSILLA *(cutting in)* So who's going to look at him? I mean – I could do it, but—

ROBERT Leave it to me. I don't know much, but it shouldn't be too difficult to see if he's still breathing. Does anyone have a mirror?

PHILLIPA There's a compact in my bag. I'll come up with you.

ROBERT *(doubtfully)* There's no need.

PHILLIPA *(taking a deep breath)* After what's happened here already, I don't think another corpse is going to unsettle me. I've been writing about them for years. *(looking at* ANTHONY*)* But I think Mr Strickland should have a drink or two. He looks like he's going to faint.

ANTHONY *(shaking his head weakly)* I'm all right. Really, I am.

ROBERT It shouldn't take long.

ROBERT *exits, followed by* PHILLIPA.

DRUSILLA *(to* ANTHONY*)* How about a nice cup of tea?

She lifts the cup and saucer from HECUBA'*s tray.*

HECUBA *(startled)* But it's... *(catching herself)* probably cold by now.

DRUSILLA *(mildly)* Then I'd better make some fresh, hadn't I? *(replacing the cup and saucer and taking the tray from her)* Come along, Mr Strickland. *(crossing to the door)* You can help me in the kitchen.

ANTHONY *stands unsteadily, and moves towards* DRUSILLA. *She exits the room and he follows her out meekly.*

CICELY *(rising, hurrying to the doors, closing them, then turning to face* HECUBA; *hissing furtively)* What the hell's going on, Hecuba? *(rising)* Why kill Sir Beverley?

HECUBA *(protesting)* But I didn't. *(puzzled)* It must have been natural causes.

CICELY *(scornfully)* In this house? There hasn't been a natural death here since Septimus died. *(puzzled)* But if you didn't do it, it must have been Drusilla. *(moving down left; thinking)* Or big brother, Postumus. *(curiously)* Where is he, by the way? I can't wait to meet him.

HECUBA *(distractedly)* Away on business.

CICELY *(frowning)* I thought the family never left the place.

HECUBA *(still preoccupied)* They didn't. Not in the old days. Except for Septimus, of course. He couldn't risk the rest of them running round loose. They were quite mad, you know. *(primly)* Not at all like our side of the family. *(focusing on* CICELY) But since Vesta inherited, I've never known where anyone was. Or what they're doing. *(stung)* I'm not one of them, you see. The actual family. *(bitterly)* I'm just an outsider who no one wants to recognize. If I want to know anything, I have to find out for myself.

CICELY *(frustrated)* So you wouldn't know what Sir Beverley was really doing here? *(scornfully)* He didn't fool me with his "taking a break" story. A day off would have killed him. He was more a workaholic than I am.

HECUBA *(dismissively)* Oh, I knew why he was here, all right. *(scornfully)* He was threatening to blackmail us.

CICELY *reacts in surprise.*

That's why Drusilla asked me to deal with him. One sip of the Captain Bligh, and he'd never have bothered us again.

CICELY *(drily)* Well, he certainly won't now. *(puzzled)* But what's Captain Bligh?

HECUBA *(beaming)* One of my own poisons. It's made from Akee fruit. The *Blighia sapida*. Named after Captain Bligh. I import them from Africa and distil the poison in Lucien's old laboratory. It causes wonderful convulsions and it's so easy to use. There's bottles of it in the dispensary. *(objecting)* But it couldn't have been Drusilla who killed Sir Beverley. She never left the room. And as for Posti...

CICELY *(frowning)* Then maybe the Collins woman is right. If Sir Beverley hasn't died of natural causes, there is another killer in the house. *(puzzled)* But which of them is it?

HECUBA *(staring at her, then blinking; suddenly)* The actress. The one you've taken upstairs.

CICELY *(blankly)* Miranda Torrence?

HECUBA *(eyes narrowing)* She's no more Miranda Torrence than I am. *(firmly)* She's Monica Tomb. *(babbling)* I thought she looked familiar the minute I saw her.

CICELY But—

HECUBA I'd never met her, of course. There was no love lost between her side of the family and Vesta's. I just thought my eyes were playing tricks. But now I know I'm right. *(firmly)* You can't mistake a Tomb. The nose and cheekbones always give them away. *(remembering)* And she's kept the same initials. M.T.

CICELY *(puzzled)* But if she is Monica Tomb, then what's she doing back here? And who's the man with her?

HECUBA *(mind racing)* Just an accomplice, I expect. Someone to throw us off the scent. But as for why she's back, it's as plain as the nose on your face. She's heard we've inherited the house, and as Septimus's only surviving child, she could never allow that to happen. *(horrified)* She'll kill all of us to get her hands on it.

CICELY But surely she'd be recognized by someone? The minute she showed her face.

HECUBA *(shaking her head)* Everyone who knew her is dead. She could live here for the rest of her life and no one would be any the wiser. That's why she's killing the others first. So the news can't get out that she's back in England and hiding in Monument House.

She presses her fist to her lips.

CICELY *(uncertainly)* But there's nothing to worry about, is there? I mean – the bed will take care of her – and her accomplice. Drusilla said so. Didn't she?

HECUBA *(still worried)* Yes. But we didn't realize who she was, then. There isn't a hope she'll turn off the bedside lights, now. She knows all the house's secrets. *(agitated)* I must warn the children. You've no idea how dangerous she is.

She heads for the door.

CICELY *(hastily)* Wait.

HECUBA *stops and turns.*

(moving quickly to her) If Miranda Torrence is Monica Tomb, then why not deal with her yourself? Before giving them the chance? As you said earlier, they don't have much respect for your capabilities, so why not show them you're not the nobody they think you are?

HECUBA *(considers this; brightening)* You're right. And I could use the Cytisine, couldn't I? *(nodding to herself)* I'm sure there's some of it left. *(to CICELY)* Quite appropriate, wouldn't you say?

CICELY *(blankly)* I'm sorry?

HECUBA *(explaining)* For having the last laugh. It's one of the symptoms of Cytisine, you see. Once it's taken effect, even the lightest touch feels like someone's tickling you.

You could say she'll giggle herself to death. *(beaming)* Oh, Cicely. I knew I could rely on you.

HECUBA *hurries out, happily.*

CICELY *(gazing after her, then shaking her head in disbelief; to herself)* She's even madder than I thought she was. *(smiling coldly)* Still...it'll be one less to deal with. Then five more to go, and it'll be champagne all the way

She moves to the drinks table and pours herself a glass of brandy.

PHILLIPA *enters behind her, looking grim.*

PHILLIPA *(flatly)* He was right.

Startled, **CICELY** *turns to her.*

Sir Beverley is dead.

CICELY *(feigning shock)* Oh, my God.

She puts her glass down on the drinks table.

PHILLIPA *(moving down left of the settee)* Which makes three bodies in almost as many hours.

CICELY How awful.

PHILLIPA *(sitting on the settee)* It's like something from a television drama. One accidental death...and two, rather badly disguised murders. Oh, yes. There's no mistake. Mr Danesworth didn't kill himself. I can easily prove that. And Sir Beverley didn't die from any asthma attack. *(off-handedly)* It's one of the advantages of being a writer. We're always researching. I don't suppose you've read my *Coffins for Two*, but one of the characters in that was killed off by an induced asthma attack, so I knew what to look for the minute we got to his room. There was no discolouration. No blue lips. Nothing.

CICELY *(frowning)* Then...?

PHILLIPA I wouldn't have seen it at all if we hadn't tried to move him to the bed. He'd been injected with something. There was the tiniest little puncture mark on the back of his neck.

She indicates on herself.

CICELY *(protesting)* But – that could have been a mosquito bite. Heaven knows there's enough of them buzzing round this place.

PHILLIPA *(shaking her head)* I don't think so. There was a faint smell of something odd, in the room. Like nail polish remover. I just wish I could remember what it reminded me of. But the police will work it out when they arrive. We're going for them as soon as Mr Sandbrooke's checked on his wife. My coat's in the hall.

CICELY *(concerned)* But what about the gunman? The one Mr Strickland saw?

PHILLIPA We've only his word for that.

CICELY *(puzzled)* I'm sorry?

PHILLIPA *(mildly)* He could have killed Sir Beverley himself. It doesn't take a genius to work it out. They were already here when the rest of us arrived, so who else could it have been? You don't go round killing perfect strangers. Not in my experience. If this were one of my books, it'd be an open and shut case.

DRUSILLA *enters.*

DRUSILLA What would?

She moves centre, behind settee.

CICELY Sir Beverley's death. She thinks he was murdered.

DRUSILLA *(staring at* PHILLIPA, *disdainfully)* Are you sure you're feeling all right? Five minutes ago you were claiming Mr Danesworth hadn't killed himself. Now it's Sir Beverley who's been murdered.

PHILLIPA And who knows who's next? I'd feel safer being stalked by the Norfolk Strangler.

ROBERT *appears in the doorway. He is in his topcoat again.*

ROBERT Ready when you are, Ms Collins.

PHILLIPA *rises and moves up to him.*

DRUSILLA *(surprised)* Where are you going?

ROBERT To fetch the police. If someone doesn't get their finger out, the house'll be full of bodies by tomorrow. And I don't intend one of them to be mine.

PHILLIPA Hear, hear.

DRUSILLA *(tightly)* Well, I'm terribly sorry, but this is a respectable hotel and though the sooner we get the police here the better, we're not having them brought out on the word of an obviously deranged writer of trashy crime novels.

She glares at **PHILLIPA**.

ROBERT *(heavily)* I'm afraid you haven't much choice, Miss Tomb. Like it or not, they'll be tearing this place apart in the next few hours. Somebody killed Sir Beverley – and possibly Danesworth, too, so you'd better get used to the idea.

DRUSILLA *(fuming)* This is ridiculous.

ROBERT *(about to leave)* And by the way – Miranda's on her way down. She'll be keeping an eye on things till we're back, so you'd better let the rest know that if they're thinking of slipping away before that happens, I wouldn't recommend it. She's not the pushover most of you seem to think she is.

ROBERT *exits, followed by* **PHILLIPA**.

DRUSILLA *hesitates, then begins to follow them.*

CICELY *(hastily)* Drusilla.

DRUSILLA *halts and looks at her.*

I know you don't trust me, but there's something I have to tell you. Something important. But you've got to promise you didn't hear it from me.

Behind DRUSILLA, *the panel begins to open.*

DRUSILLA *(tightly)* Go on.

CICELY It's about— *(She notices the panel and stops in mid sentence.)*

DRUSILLA *(impatiently)* Well?

A gloved hand emerges, clutching a gun.

As CICELY *continues to gape,* DRUSILLA *realizes and turns to face the panel.*

(startled) What are you doing? I told you not to—

The gun fires and DRUSILLA *staggers, then with a surprised look on her face, drops to the floor. As* CICELY *reacts, the gun is tossed into the room and the panel closes again. Cautiously,* CICELY *approaches the body and touches it gingerly before picking up the gun.*

As CICELY *stares at it,* ANTHONY *hurries in.*

ANTHONY *(aghast)* Oh, my God.

He recoils and holds up his hands in surrender.

CICELY *(unwittingly aiming the gun at him)* She's been shot. From inside there.

She indicates the panel.

MIRANDA *hurries in.*

MIRANDA What's happened? *(seeing* DRUSILLA *and reacting)* Ohhhhh.

She rushes forward and wrestles the gun from CICELY's *hand.*

CICELY *backs to the drinks table.*

HECUBA *hurries in.*

HECUBA *(anxiously)* Who was that shooting? I won't allow guns in— *(seeing the body)* Drusilla. *(reacting, then hissing furiously to* MIRANDA*)* What have you done, you stupid woman?

MIRANDA *(protesting)* It wasn't me.

HECUBA *(indignantly)* That carpet is priceless. It'll need scrubbing to get the stains out.

ROBERT *and* PHILLIPA *enter, looking concerned.*

ROBERT We heard a shot... *(seeing the body)* Oh, my God. *(looking at* MIRANDA*)* Miranda???

MIRANDA *(faintly)* Somebody's killed her. With this.

She shows the gun.

HECUBA *(tartly)* Yes. And we all know who did it. She did. *(glaring at* MIRANDA*)* Monica Tomb.

ANTHONY *(staring at* MIRANDA*)* Monica???

Everyone looks at her.

ROBERT *(defensively)* Don't be ridiculous. Of course she's not Monica Tomb. She's not Monica anybody, let alone a bloody serial killer. She wouldn't hurt a fly. *(to* MIRANDA*)* Would you, darling?

ANTHONY *(to* MIRANDA*)* Is it true? Is your name really Monica?

MIRANDA *(uncomfortable)* I don't know how she guessed, but yes. It's the name I was christened with.

They all stare at her.

Lights fade.

Scene Two

The same. An hour later.

DRUSILLA'*s body has been removed. The door is open.*
PHILLIPA *stands centre, between the settee and the wing*
chair, loosely holding the gun. **MIRANDA** *and* **ROBERT**
are on the settee. **HECUBA** *sits in the wing chair, with*
CICELY *standing to the right of her, brandy glass in*
hand. **ANTHONY** *is standing down left, his back to the*
rest of them. All look shaken.

PHILLIPA *(to* **CICELY***)* So, the panel opened... Someone shot
Drusilla, then threw this *(brandishing the gun)* into the
room and you picked it up?

CICELY *nods.*

A bit on the stupid side, wouldn't you say?

CICELY *(stung)* I didn't think. I was in shock.

PHILLIPA *(to* **MIRANDA***)* Then you came in and snatched it
off her?

MIRANDA *(weakly)* I thought she was going to shoot again.

ROBERT At Strickland.

He indicates him with his head.

PHILLIPA *(to* **ROBERT***)* And just to confuse matters further, you
took it from her. Which means that as far as fingerprints
are concerned, it may just as well have been wiped clean.
(sighing) Amateurs.

She puts it on the table behind the settee.

ROBERT *(annoyed)* All right, Miss Marple. We're not all crime-
writers. Miranda had never touched a gun in her life, and
it could have still been loaded. The sooner I got it away
from her, the less chance she had of firing it by accident.

(pointedly) And you seem to forget that you've been waving it around like a fairy wand for the past ten minutes.

CICELY *(peeved)* Besides...I've already told you, whoever killed Drusilla, was wearing gloves. There wouldn't have been any fingerprints.

She takes a drink from her glass.

PHILLIPA *(ignoring her and frowning)* But the real puzzle is, what was the point of throwing it in here? It doesn't make sense.

ANTHONY *(turning to her)* They could have hoped whoever picked it up would provide prints.

PHILLIPA *(shaking her head)* No, no. You don't understand. It doesn't make sense, because the gun we have here *(indicating it)* isn't the right one.

All look at PHILLIPA *strangely.*

HECUBA *(frowning)* Right one?

PHILLIPA Well...you've all said you've never seen it before.

CICELY So?

PHILLIPA *(explaining)* It's nothing at all like the one Mr Strickland saw the man in the drive carrying. Remember? That was a magnum. The Dirty Harry gun. *(realizing)* Sorry. I forgot. You weren't here, were you? It happened about an hour ago. It's why he didn't get to the village. He came back to warn us.

ANTHONY *nods.*

ROBERT *(stunned)* And you never told us? *(annoyed)* I don't believe this. Bodies dropping like flies, and the last to know there's a madman on the prowl are the ones who should have known first. *(incredulously)* What's wrong with you people? We're supposed to be on our honeymoon.

He tightens his grip on MIRANDA.

CICELY *(to* PHILLIPA*)* So what you're saying is – if he was carrying a magnum, why kill Drusilla with that?

She indicates the gun with her head.

PHILLIPA Exactly.

ANTHONY *(helpfully)* Perhaps he had two guns?

PHILLIPA *(exasperated)* Oh, if only Hermione Pink was here. *(explaining)* She's the detective in all my books. She'd work it out in a flash. *(heaving a deep sigh)* So, what else do we know?

HECUBA *(glaring at* MIRANDA*)* We know that she's here under false pretences. *(bitterly)* Why couldn't she have been shot instead of Drusilla? And she's not convinced me she's not Monica Tomb.

ROBERT *(hotly)* Well, it's clear enough to me. The name of Monica Snodgrass is hardly likely to draw West End audiences, so what's wrong with changing it to Miranda Torrence? *(pulling* MIRANDA *closer to him)* There're thousands of performers working under names they weren't born with.

PHILLIPA *(to* HECUBA*)* And writers. It's not uncommon, Mrs Tomb.

HECUBA *(stubbornly)* She still shouldn't be here. None of you should. *(bitterly)* We'd nothing like this in Monument House till you all arrived.

ROBERT *(glaring at her)* Well, like it or not, we are here. And it looks like we've no choice but to stay till the fog's cleared and the maniac doing the killings decides to call it a day. I'm not venturing out till I can damn well see where I'm going.

MIRANDA*'s eyelids begin to droop.*

CICELY *(anxiously)* And what if he doesn't call it a day?

They all look unhappy at the thought.

ANTHONY *(uneasily)* He can't want to kill us all. What would his motive be? Most of us hadn't met till tonight.

PHILLIPA *(mildly)* Perhaps he just likes killing?

ROBERT *(irritated)* We're not in one of your books, Ms Collins. You don't go round bumping strangers off in real life. *(frustrated)* And where the hell's he hiding himself?

CICELY *(uneasily)* Could be anywhere. As Mr Danesworth said – you could hide an army inside this place.

HECUBA *(firmly)* Rubbish. Monument House was built for the Tomb family. What would they want with hidden rooms and secret passages?

PHILLIPA *(pointedly)* You've certainly got one.

MIRANDA *yawns sleepily.*

HECUBA *(acidly)* Which was probably a servants' entrance in the days before Septimus Tomb converted the dining room into his library. *(standing)* Now if you don't mind, I need to lie down. This terrible murder's quite upset me and my head is pounding. Please turn out the lights before retiring. The last bill they sent was criminal.

HECUBA *exits.*

ROBERT *(aghast)* She must be joking. I don't care if her bill goes through the roof. We're leaving every light on till it's clear enough to see where we're going, then we're out of here like bats from hell.

CICELY And what do we do in the meantime? We can't stay here just staring at each other.

ROBERT I don't see why not. We're safer here than anywhere else in the bloody place.

CICELY And what about your wife? I'm not exactly an expert, but she looks about ready to drop.

MIRANDA *(pathetically)* I am feeling tired, Bobby.

CICELY It could be shock again. I suggest you take her upstairs and let her get a decent night's sleep. The rest of us will keep our eyes open.

ROBERT *(looking at* MIRANDA, *who nods weakly; reluctantly)* All right, then. But in case anyone's interested, I've no intention of sleeping myself. The door'll be locked, and if anyone even breathes on the other side of it, they'll soon find out they've made a big mistake.

He rises and assists MIRANDA *to stand.*

MIRANDA *(forcing a smile)* 'Night.

They move around the settee and head for the door.

CICELY Wait. *(crossing to the table behind the settee and picking up the dish of Turkish Delight)* You'd better take this.

ROBERT *looks at it in bewilderment.*

In case of emergencies.

ROBERT Oh.

He takes it from her with a frown.

ROBERT *exits with* MIRANDA.

CICELY *(to* PHILLIPA*)* Low blood sugar. Diabetes, so he told me.

PHILLIPA *(sympathetically)* Poor man.

CICELY *(quickly)* No, no. Not him. Her. That's why she fainted earlier. Forgot to take her dose, or something.

PHILLIPA I see.

CICELY *(briskly)* Well, I don't know about you two, but I could do with another drink. *(crossing to the drinks table)* Anyone care to join me?

ANTHONY *(shaking his head)* Not for me, thanks. I'm more of a tea man. *(doubtfully)* Do you think Mrs Tomb'd mind if I made myself a brew?

PHILLIPA *(firmly)* What the eye doesn't see, the heart doesn't grieve about. I think I'll join you. If there is a madman roaming the house, I want my wits about me before he gets a chance to show off his shooting skills.

CICELY *(frowning)* Wouldn't we be better all staying together? You know what they say about safety in numbers?

ANTHONY It'll only take a minute or two.

PHILLIPA *(firmly)* Which gives him plenty of time to blow a hole through your brain if he takes the notion. I'll come with you.

CICELY And what about me?

PHILLIPA *(picking up the gun)* By the weight of it, there's still a few bullets left in here. *(holding it out to her)* If you see a face you don't recognize, just point it at him and pull the trigger till the damned thing's empty.

CICELY *(stunned)* I couldn't. I've never fired a gun in my life.

PHILLIPA Neither have I. But I wouldn't just stand there to be murdered if a gun was in my hand. He'd have more holes in him than a net curtain. *(putting the gun down again)* But you needn't worry. I don't think he's after you. As a matter of fact, I'm finally starting to see where all this is leading.

ANTHONY *(puzzled)* You are?

PHILLIPA *(convinced)* Oh, yes. I'm not a writer for nothing. It's just a case of putting all the odd clues in the right order, and the answer'll stare you in the face. Most crimes are solved by listening to what people actually say...and I've heard some very interesting things in the last two hours. Waiting for the kettle to boil'll just give me time to check if I'm right. Ten more minutes and this'll all be behind us.

PHILLIPA *exits.*

ANTHONY *(glancing at* **CICELY** *in a puzzled manner)* I wish I was as confident as she is. *(picking up the gun)* But if you're not going to use this, I think I'll borrow it. Better safe than sorry.

ANTHONY *follows* PHILLIPA *out.*

CICELY *hurries to the internal phone. She dials a number, impatiently waits for a reply, then hangs up. She's frustrated.*

CICELY Damn.

She moves back to the drinks table, pours herself a brandy and takes a huge gulp. Refilling the glass, she moves aimlessly around, sipping at it, a worried expression on her face.

ROBERT *appears again and enters.*

ROBERT I don't suppose anyone's got a... *(He realizes the room is empty but for* CICELY, *and stops speaking.)*

CICELY *(turning rapidly to face him)* Where the hell have you been? *(angrily hissing)* I've been trying to call you. We may have a problem.

ROBERT *(staring at her for a moment, then closing the door behind him and lowering his voice)* What are you talking about?

CICELY *(tightly)* The Collins woman. I think she's worked out what we're up to.

ROBERT *(after a moment; scornfully)* How could she? She's fifty pence short of a pound.

He moves behind the settee.

CICELY *(savagely)* But smart enough to realize that Danesworth didn't kill himself and Comstock hadn't died of an athsma attack.

She takes another gulp of her drink.

ROBERT *(reasonably)* But how could she know we're involved? As far as she knows, we only met tonight. And besides, she'll be dead before morning, so what the hell's it matter? *(frowning)* The thing that worries me is who it was Strickland saw in the drive? The man with the gun.

CICELY *(surprised)* I thought that was you.

ROBERT *(amused)* Come on, sweetie. What would I do with a gun? I couldn't hit a barn door at five paces.

CICELY *(puzzled)* Then who shot Drusilla?

ROBERT *(frowning)* I thought you did. *(puzzled)* Didn't you?

CICELY *(realizing)* Oh, my God. She was right, after all.

ROBERT Who was?

CICELY *(moving up to him and putting her glass down on the table behind the settee)* Hecuba. You idiot. That little tart you married is Monica Tomb.

ROBERT *(shaking his head)* No, she's not. She's a two-bit actress who inherits a fortune when dear old Daddy's will's gone through probate. Why do you think I married her? It wasn't for intellectual stimulus. She's thicker than two short planks.

CICELY *(scornfully)* And you're Albert Einstein, of course? *(furiously)* She's Monica Tomb, I tell you, and you've brought her back here to screw up the biggest scam we've ever attempted. *(seething)* Why was I stupid enough to get you involved?

She turns her back to him.

ROBERT *(snapping)* Because you couldn't pull this off on your own, that's why. *(grabbing her and turning her to face him)* All right. So what if she is Monica Tomb? What difference would it make?

CICELY *shakes herself free with annoyance.*

I don't know what you replaced her insulin with, but she's so groggy now, she can hardly walk. If I turned off the bedside lamp, there isn't a chance she wouldn't suffocate.

That's what you told me, isn't it? The canopy comes down? (*frowning*) And what was all that with the Turkish Delight?

CICELY (*recovering herself*) Just another precaution. Hecuba's dusted it with antimony. Feed your Purple-Green Pony that if she has another attack and she'll be out of our hair for good.

She moves right.

ROBERT (*following*) But what about the money? You said we wouldn't kill her unless we absolutely had to. And if she's not Monica Tomb, I'd lose out on thousands.

CICELY (*harshly*) Once the Tombs are dead, we'll have so much money we won't know what to do with it. (*turning to face him*) Have you any idea how much a Hassock house is worth to us? According to the late (*sneering*) Mr Danesworth, with careful handling of the media, we could be talking millions. And that's just in this country.

ROBERT And you're sure he knew what he was talking about?

CICELY (*smirking*) He may have been an old queen, but when it came to Hassock, no one knew more about him than Danesworth. He was a walking encyclopaedia. Why do you think I told him about this place?

She turns away and moves down right.

ROBERT But how did you know about it?

CICELY (*not looking at him*) It was mentioned in Hecuba's book of family memoirs. She showed it to me just after they moved in. When he turned up asking questions, last month, I remembered we had the original deeds in the firm's vaults, and dug them out. (*smiling at the memory*) It was the best move I ever made. Get rid of the Tombs, and Monument House was mine.

ROBERT (*following her down*) But why drag him down here?

CICELY (*facing right*) Because Vesta wouldn't let me near the place when she was alive, and knowing how sheeplike the Tombs were, the rest of them would keep up the tradition. My

only chance of getting a foot in the door was by pretending
to warn Hecuba that Danesworth was sniffing around, then
finishing them off before they knew what had hit them.
That's why I drove him down here and waited till he made
himself known, before making my own appearance.

ROBERT (*frowning*) Must have been a shock to find the place
full of strangers. Especially old Comstock. What the hell
was he doing here?

ROBERT *casually touches* CICELY'*s arm and she giggles.*

(*surprised*) What?

CICELY (*turning to him in annoyance*) Will you stop doing
that? You know I hate being tickled.

ROBERT *spreads his hands in bewilderment.*

(*staring at him; realizing*) Oh, my God. No. (*wildly*)
Noooooo.

ROBERT (*startled*) What is it?

CICELY The poison. The one she was going to kill Monica with.
She's given it to me.

She giggles helplessly.

ROBERT (*baffled*) What are you talking about? Who has?

CICELY (*screeching*) Hecuba, you idiot. (*giggling*) She's poisoned
me. She's poisoned me.

*She laughs helplessly for a few moments, then falls to the
floor in a crumpled heap.*

ROBERT (*staring at her body*) Cicely? Cis?

He backs away from her.

The door opens and HECUBA *enters in nightgown and
dressing gown.*

HECUBA *(crossly)* Will you please keep the noise down? Some of us are trying to—

ROBERT *(rushing upstage and grabbing her)* What have you done, you old bitch? What have you done?

HECUBA *(blankly)* What? *(seeing the body and reacts)* Cicely?

She attempts to pass him to reach CICELY.

ROBERT *(retaining his grip; angrily)* She said you'd poisoned her. And couldn't stop laughing about it.

HECUBA *(in disbelief)* But that's impossible. *(pulling free)* The only poison that makes people laugh before they die is Cytisine and we're completely out of it. I know that because I looked for it less than an hour ago and only found the empty jar. *(realizing)* We use it for – for – *(rapidly thinking)* pest control. *(primly)* Much better than all those nasty traps in the cellars. Besides...it's hardly ever used on humans these days. It doesn't work fast enough.

ROBERT *(still angry)* Well, it certainly did this time. One minute she was fine, and the next...

He looks at the body.

HECUBA *(pained)* But why did she say I'd poisoned her? Cicely was my friend.

ROBERT *(snarling)* Yes. And with friends like you, she certainly didn't need enemies.

HECUBA *(affronted)* That's a very offensive remark, Mr Sandbrooke. And unless you apologize at once, you can go wherever your so-called wife is going at the moment, and never come back.

She turns to exit.

ROBERT *(startled)* What are you talking about? Miranda's in bed and out to the world. She's not going anywhere.

HECUBA *(turning back)* Really? Then who did I see through the landing window a few moments ago, hurrying down the drive with a case in her hand?

ROBERT *stares at her, then hurries out past her and vanishes from sight.*

(moving to CICELY *and stooping to shake her)* It's all right, dear. You can stop pretending. I've sent him on a wild goose chase.

There is no movement from CICELY.

(uncertainly) Cicely?

She examines her more closely then straightens, looks puzzled, then crosses to the drinks table and opens the brandy bottle to sniff at the contents. With an odd look on her face, she stands immobile, then turns to the door.

ANTHONY *enters, carrying the gun carelessly by the barrel.*

Oh, Posti. Thank goodness you're back.

ANTHONY Why? *(seeing* CICELY'*s body and reacting)* What happened?

HECUBA *(flustered)* I knew she'd have to be killed, when she mentioned Caligula's bed. You see, she wasn't in the room when Drusilla told Sir Beverley how it worked, so that meant she must have been listening behind the panel and had something to do with the other deaths. *(bitterly)* Oh, Posti... I'm so sorry. You and Drusilla were right. I was silly to trust her and it was all my fault she wormed her way into the house. *(distraught)* How can you forgive me?

ANTHONY *(drily)* I shouldn't worry about it, Aunt Heck. I had my own suspicions when she mentioned this place was the site of Danesworth's greatest discovery. How would she know that when she'd supposedly never met him before?

(frowning) But why kill her here? If one of the others walks in—

HECUBA *(impatiently)* But that's what I'm trying to tell you. It wasn't me who did it. And there's Cytisine in the brandy.

She displays the bottle.

ANTHONY *(puzzled)* But we haven't used Cytisine in years. *(putting the gun on the table behind the settee)* Are you sure?

HECUBA Of course I am. And there's something else with it. Oleander, I think.

ANTHONY *(thoughtfully)* Then if you didn't poison the brandy, the Collins woman was right. She explained it all in the kitchen. There has to be more than one killer in the house. *(grimly)* And apart from my wholly fictitious gunman, there's not many suspects left. Mr and Mrs Sandbrooke, and—

HECUBA *(cutting in)* The Collins woman herself. We mustn't forget her.

She puts the brandy bottle back on the drinks table.

ANTHONY *(shaking his head)* No, no, Aunt Heck. She couldn't have killed any of the others. She was never in the right place. But I had to deal with her, just to be on the safe side. She's in the chest freezer with Aggie Hammond's meat cleaver lodged in the back of her head. So as I was saying, it's just a question of who's the most likely suspect? Mr, or Mrs?

HECUBA *(firmly)* It's her, of course. Cousin Monica. I told you she was back. *(worried)* We don't stand a chance against her.

ANTHONY If Miranda Torrence was Monica Tomb, I'd quite agree. But she's not. Her eyes are brown. Hadn't you noticed? Mendel's law. Blue-eyed parents can't produce brown-eyed children, and Grandpa and Grandma Tomb had eyes the colour of sapphires. *(decisively)* No. The woman's exactly what Sandbrooke said she was – an actress. I'll bet my life that he's the one we're after. We can dispose of her the minute we've done with him. Where is he, by the way?

HECUBA Halfway down the drive, I expect, but he'll be back as soon as he realizes I've sent him on a wild goose chase.

ANTHONY Then we'd better get ready for him.

HECUBA *(glancing at* CICELY*)* And what about her?

ANTHONY *(decisively)* Behind the bookcase. Before he gets back.

He moves to open it.

HECUBA *(puzzled)* But why? He already knows she's dead.

ANTHONY *(opening the panel)* Catch up, Aunt Heck. You've always wanted to be a Tomb, so start to think like one. We tell him she had some kind of fit, but now she's come round and gone to her room to tidy herself up. He'll be so confused, we can finish him off before he has a chance to catch us off guard.

He moves towards her.

They carry CICELY's *body into the passage, they emerge again.*

HECUBA *moves down right as* ANTHONY *closes the panel.*

HECUBA *(relaxing)* Oh, Posti. I should have known you'd have everything under control. You always were the one with brains.

She beams.

ANTHONY *(moving left in front of the settee)* Yes. But if I hadn't been preoccupied with making sure Sir Beverley couldn't pull the rug from under our feet, none of this would have happened, and Dru would still be here.

HECUBA *(primly)* Well, that's what comes of keeping secrets from us. You were away for weeks and we'd no idea where you'd gone. Drusilla was worried sick.

ANTHONY *(turning to her)* What else could I do? The minute I heard private detectives had been asking questions about Athene's whereabouts, I'd no choice but to get rid of them.

And when I found out who was behind the enquiries, I'd
to work even faster. We'd never been tracked before and
our sensible customers knew better than to try it. But Sir
Beverley was a different matter. If he knew where to find
us, he could blackmail us into doing disposals for him, free
of charge. Refuse...and he was rich and clever enough to
drop us in the soup without getting himself splashed.

HECUBA So you went to London and took a job with his firm?

ANTHONY *(nodding)* He was always wanting PAs. Went through
them like a dose of salts. A few faked references and the
job was mine. Just in time, too. When he mentioned he
was heading up country the following day on a top-secret
mission, I guessed he was making his move, so I slipped
his chauffeur something to make sure he was in no fit state
to drive and volunteered for the job myself. Far easier to
dispose of His Highness in the marshes than the middle of
London. But when the rest of them turned up, it became a
lot more complicated.

HECUBA *(peevishly)* Then why invite them to stay?

ANTHONY *(patiently)* Because they knew he was here, and
when the news broke about his disappearance, one of them
might have remembered, opened their mouth, and brought
the police looking in this direction. We had to silence them
all before that had a chance to happen. *(grimacing)* But
Sandbrooke beat us to it and we still don't know why. Though
I intend to find out.

MIRANDA *enters the room unsteadily. She wears a silky
dressing gown over her nightdress, and soft slippers.*

MIRANDA *(faintly)* Robert. I want Robert.

She staggers to behind the settee.

HECUBA *(feigning concern)* Of course you do, dear. He'll be
back in a moment. *(fussily)* But let me pour you a brandy.
You look terrible.

She moves to the drinks table and picks up the brandy bottle.

MIRANDA *(weakly)* No, no. You don't have to bother.

Her persona undergoes a complete change as she snatches up the gun, points it at HECUBA *and speaks harshly.*

I can't say I'm fond of Cytisine. Especially mixed with half a dozen other poisons and nasty, cheap alcohol.

As HECUBA *turns to her in shock,* MIRANDA *backs up to the fireplace, the gun covering both* HECUBA *and* ANTHONY.

(smiling) Sorry about that, but I really do prefer a good champagne.

ANTHONY *(looking puzzled)* What are you talking about?

MIRANDA *(pityingly)* Poor Mr Strickland. You hadn't a clue what was going on, had you? *(Kindly)* But I shouldn't feel too badly about it. Neither did the rest of them. We're a very good team. Bobby and me.

HECUBA *(shocked)* You mean – you're in it together?

ANTHONY *(still playing the innocent)* In what? I don't understand.

MIRANDA *(to him; kindly)* Of course you don't. So why don't you sit, and let me explain?

She motions with the gun towards the settee.

ANTHONY *moves to it warily and sits down left.* MIRANDA *nods towards the wing chair and* HECUBA *reluctantly sits in it.*

That's better. *(mockingly; moving forward to position herself above and between them)* Are we all comfortable? *(smiling coldly)* Then I'll begin. *(lightly)* We were having some rather unpleasant financial problems, chez Sandbrooke, when Bobby got the call from Miss Venner. Quite out of the blue, it came. He hadn't heard from her in years. Not since he left London because of a misunderstanding with the Fraud Squad, and had to change his name from Bonnington to Sandbrooke.

HECUBA *(surprised)* Bonnington? You mean – he used to be married to her?

MIRANDA *(mockingly)* Oh, my. Aren't we the clever one? There's not much gets past you, is there, Mrs Tomb?

ANTHONY *(blankly)* Then if they used to be married, why pretend they'd never met before?

ROBERT *enters and moves to centre of the settee back.*

ROBERT *(confidently smirking)* Because she wanted me to do a job for her, and the fewer who knew about our past relationship, the easier it'd be.

HECUBA *(glowering)* And what exactly was this mysterious job?

ROBERT *(smiling)* She'd found out from Danesworth that this place was worth a king's ransom, and needed help to dispose of him and get her grubby little hands on it.

HECUBA *(indignantly)* I don't believe a word. We'd never sell Monument House.

MIRANDA *(drily)* Did anyone mention buying it? Once he'd helped her dispose of Danesworth and the Tombs, she'd inherit everything. Lock, stock and barrel. And more to the point, we'd be richer by a million pounds.

ANTHONY *(as though puzzled)* But how? She wasn't one of the family, was she?

MIRANDA *(amused)* Never heard of forgery, Mr Strickland? Bobby's quite an expert. Particularly with wills. *(to ROBERT)* Aren't you, darling?

ROBERT *attempts to look modest.*

ANTHONY *(still pretending to be shocked)* So...you came here to kill the Tombs? It wasn't by accident at all?

ROBERT *(amused)* The only accident involved was that idiot writer's friend waltzing off with my laptop by mistake. The whole plan was inside it. If they opened it up, we were all for the high jump. We had to get the damn thing back and ended up chasing them miles.

MIRANDA We couldn't believe our luck when they turned in here. Not that it made things easier. We expected the place to be empty. Except for the Tombs and Danesworth, of course.

ROBERT Gave me quite a shock when I found out Sir Beverley was here. The one man who could have recognized me, and ended the scam before it began.

ANTHONY So you killed him?

MIRANDA *(lightly)* No, actually. Despite his tough man image, he's rather squeamish when it comes to murder, *(to ROBERT)* aren't you, dear? *(to ANTHONY again)* His best work's always been done with a pen. It was Cicely who finished Sir Beverley off. With the insulin from my kit. *(brightly)* I really do have diabetes, but Bobby made quite sure I never injected myself with whatever she replaced it with.

She simpers.

ANTHONY *(in a puzzled voice)* But if you were all in it together—?

MIRANDA Why would she want to harm me? *(smiling)* Because Miss oh-so-clever-and-efficient Venner had no idea that Bobby was double-crossing her. As far as she was concerned, I was just a dizzy blonde to be disposed of the minute the job was over. She never dreamed that I'd be the one to inherit Monument House.

ROBERT *(helpfully)* We couldn't risk using my name in the will in case the police got involved and started digging. But who'd worry about a distant "cousin"?

He smiles.

HECUBA *(coldly)* And Mr Danesworth? I suppose she killed him, too?

MIRANDA *(slightly shocked)* Oh, no. I'm afraid I take the credit for that. Such an odious man. So full of his own importance. I couldn't wait to shut him up.

ANTHONY *(drily)* Or her, for that matter?

MIRANDA Of course. *(brightly)* I couldn't possibly have shared the proceeds with her, and would have dealt with her later. When everything was over. But after hiding behind the panel and hearing dear old Mrs Tomb telling her about the Cytisine she intended feeding me, I decided poetic justice might be called for. *(Smirking)* She was rather fond of brandy, the late Miss Venner. Almost an alcoholic, in my opinion, so I added it to the bottle while the rest of you were fussing over Drusilla's body.

HECUBA *(sourly)* A pity you didn't try it yourself.

MIRANDA *(amused)* There wasn't a chance of that. She'd already told Bobby the family history, so we were very careful and ate and drank nothing after getting here. As I said – we made a very good team.

ROBERT *(smiling)* And still do.

MIRANDA *(pouting)* I don't think so, precious. Not any more. I can manage the rest on my own now.

She points the gun at him and pulls the trigger.

As the others react, ROBERT *crumples to the floor, dead.*

(in tragic tones) Alas, poor Bobby. I knew him well.

ANTHONY *(gaping at the body)* You've killed him.

MIRANDA How clever of you to notice. *(with mock sorrow)* And now I'm about to kill you. Nothing pesonal in your case, darling. Under other circumstances, you'd be quite a catch, but I can't afford witnesses. *(looking at* HECUBA*)* But her. She'll be a labour of love.

HECUBA *bridles.*

(sneering) I can't wait to put a bullet through your brain. *(airily)* And as for the Collins woman, I'll finish her off the minute she shows her face.

HECUBA *(coldly)* Aren't you forgetting something? There'll still be one Tomb left. When Postumus returns...

MIRANDA *(amused)* I'll deal with him, exactly the same as you two.

She points the gun at her.

ANTHONY *(mildly)* But not with that gun.

MIRANDA *(looking at him)* Oh? And why not?

ANTHONY *(regretfully)* Because it's very difficult to pull a trigger when you're dead...and I'm afraid you began dying several minutes ago.

MIRANDA *looks puzzled.*

As my aunt can confirm, not all poisons need to be swallowed or injected. Some are absorbed through the skin. Like nicotine, or ethylene – *(pointedly)* or the one on the handle of the gun you're holding. *(smiling)* I thought one of you would pick it up, eventually. *(rising)* Postumus Tomb, by the way. Drusilla's step-brother.

MIRANDA *gapes at him, then at the gun which appears to be growing heavier, making her arm sag.*

Goodbye, Mrs Sandbrooke.

He inclines his head.

MIRANDA *(furiously)* No. *(struggling to raise the gun again, but the poison is racing through her)* No.

She drops the gun and sways.

As the others watch, her eyes roll upwards, she collapses to the floor and lies still.

HECUBA *(rising and glaring at her)* Stupid creature. No one gets the better of a Tomb. *(moving to* ANTHONY *and embracing him)* Well done, dear. I knew you'd have a trick up your sleeve. *(releasing him)* That's why Vesta favoured you so much. When Dora's gone, she'd say, "There'll be no one to touch Posti. He'll outclass the rest of us".

ANTHONY *(bitterly)* I couldn't keep Dru alive, though.

He moves left round the settee.

HECUBA *(regretfully)* Yes. That was a pity. *(brightening)* But now the others are all dead, the family's secrets are safe again. *(glaring at* MIRANDA*'s body)* And she didn't get away with it, did she?

ANTHONY *(frowning)* Away with what?

HECUBA Killing Drusilla, of course.

ANTHONY But she didn't kill Drusilla.

HECUBA *(taken aback)* Then who did?

ANTHONY *(mildly)* You did, Aunt Heck.

HECUBA *looks at him in disbelief.*

I suspected it the minute we found her. You always did resent us running the place after Gran died, and the other killings provided the perfect opportunity to dispose of us, too. Once we were out of the way, you could do what you liked with the business.

HECUBA *(aghast)* No.

ANTHONY Gran warned us to keep an eye on you after she'd gone. In fact, she made us promise not to involve you in any of the firm's disposals, and if it hadn't been for this Venner stuff distracting us, there's no way you'd have stood a chance of killing Dru.

HECUBA *(protesting)* But I didn't. It must have been one of the others.

ANTHONY *(shaking his head)* No, Aunt Heck. Sandbrooke was on the way out with the Collins woman when the shot was fired. Miranda was halfway down the stairs and I was in the kitchen. You're the only one left.

HECUBA *(blustering)* But what about Cicely. She could have—

ANTHONY *(cutting in)* Done it before killing herself with Cytisine to celebrate? I don't think so, Aunt Heck. I really don't think so. *(sadly)* Dear, dear, dear. What am I to do with you?

He advances on her with menace.

HECUBA *(realizing the game is up and her fussy demeanour is replaced by icy-cold fury; backing away right)* Do? You won't do anything, you pathetic little monster. *(sneering)* Oh, I may have been Vesta's dogsbody, for the last thirty years, but I've far more brains than anyone's ever given me credit for.

She moves behind the wing chair, and sidles down right.

ANTHONY *follows her with grim determination.*

Since the day I married into it, I studied the family's methods till I knew more about disposals than the rest of them put together. *(smugly)* And the only one who suspected a thing was Vesta. *(backing left; still facing him)* It's why she tried to kill me. *(smiling coldly)* How fortunate I was passing the kitchen and saw her spooning Salts of Lemon into the birthday cake she was making me, and how unfortunate her precious son accepted a slice from me before it had time to cool. The shock made her quite bitter, as I remember. *(sneering)* What a blessing she loved honey so much.

ANTHONY *(halting)* Honey?

HECUBA *(smugly)* On her breakfast toast. It was the last thing she ever ate. *(spitefully)* Was it my fault she was half-blind and couldn't read the label on the jar?

ANTHONY *(stunned)* You poisoned it?

HECUBA *(amused)* I didn't have to. It was one of Dora Tomb's confections. There are jars of it on the pantry shelf. She'd had her beehives right in the middle of the oleander beds, so the honey they produced would kill a horse. The only thing I did, was replace it with ordinary honey before calling you.

ANTHONY *(nodding slowly)* So Dru was right. She always suspected you'd something to do with Gran dying so suddenly.

HECUBA *(icily)* And now there's only us left. Clever little Postumus and stupid Aunt Heccie. I wonder who'll come out on top? Who will inherit Monument House?

ANTHONY *(grimly)* Well, it certainly won't be you.

He moves rapidly towards her.

She snatches a decorative pin from her hair and stabs him savagely in the wrist as he tries to grab her.

Owww.

He sucks at the wound.

HECUBA *(triumphantly)* You're not the only one with tricks up your sleeve, dear. Athene was a wonderful teacher. Thirty seconds from now, and you'll be as dead as the rest of your precious family.

ANTHONY *(looking at his hand in disbelief, then looking at her hazily; faintly)* You're wrong, Hecuba. Totally, utterly wrong.

He tries to laugh, but crumples to the floor, dead.

HECUBA *(cautiously, moving to him and examining the body; elatedly)* Wrong, am I? *(giggling madly)* Then who's still alive? Who's the last Tomb? Tell me that, will you? Who's the best of them all?

She laughs hysterically.

The panel opens and PHILLIPA *steps into the room.*

PHILLIPA *(easily)* I suppose it's a matter of opinion.

HECUBA *(turning to see her; in shock)* You? *(glancing at* ANTHONY's *body)* But he told me you were dead.

PHILLIPA *(shrugging)* As Mark Twain once said...the report of my death was greatly exaggerated. And do pull yourself together, Hecuba. A real Tomb wouldn't bat an eye after doing a disposal.

HECUBA *(still shaken)* Who are you?

PHILLIPA If you hadn't been so hasty, Posti would have told you. I'm Monica Tomb.

HECUBA *stares at her in disbelief, then raises her hair pin like a dagger and prepares to lunge.*

(frowning) I wouldn't, if I were you. You'd be dead before you knew it. *(moving down to the settee)* Now why don't you put that away and join me for a chat? You might find it interesting.

HECUBA *remains motionless.*

(reassuringly) You're quite safe. I'm not here on business.

She sits.

HECUBA *(warily)* What do you want, then? Why are you here?

PHILLIPA *(offhandedly)* It's quite simple, really. I was born in the old place, and wanted a last look round.

HECUBA *(suspiciously)* Last look?

PHILLIPA *(nodding)* There's something I have to tell you. *(hesitating, then speaking matter-of-factly)* In a few more weeks, poor old Monica Tomb will cease to exist.

HECUBA *(frowning)* I don't understand.

PHILLIPA According to the experts, my – condition – is regarded as incurable.

HECUBA *(realizing)* You mean...you're dying? *(puzzled)* But I thought you'd be wanting the house.

PHILLIPA *(wanly)* I know. Which is why I'm here, now. To tell you I couldn't care less about it. You can have it with my blessing.

HECUBA *(baffled)* But...

PHILLIPA Why didn't I contact you earlier? *(shrugging)* To tell you the truth, I couldn't stand Vesta. The most vicious and self-centred bitch I've ever come across. I didn't trust her an inch. If she patted you on the back, it was only to find the softest spot to stick a knife in.

HECUBA *(relaxing)* Oh, you're so right, dear. She was exactly the same with me. You wouldn't believe the times she humiliated me. And all I wanted was a little recognition. Not much to expect, was it? A little recognition.

PHILLIPA It was only after she died and I realized how little time I had, I decided to come back and straighten things out. But I'd never met any of you, which is why I talked Daphne into joining me for a short holiday in this area. She'd no idea who I really was, but having her with me gave me a chance to see what you were like without raising suspicions.

HECUBA *replaces her hairpin.*

And what a good job we got here in time. The mix-up with the laptops was pure coincidence, but after the first few deaths, when nothing seemed to make sense, I started fitting the pieces together.

HECUBA *(sitting beside her)* But what made you suspect the Sandbrookes?

PHILLIPA Simple. When you accused Miranda of being me, he didn't have to ask who I was.

HECUBA *(puzzled)* But why would that make...

PHILLIPA *(patiently)* Because he must have already known. Someone had told him about me. And who could that have been? The only outsider who knew the family well enough was Cicely Venner, which indicated she was in on the killings, too. And then there was Danesworth.

HECUBA What about him?

PHILLIPA When he first met you, he called you Mrs Tomb. As no one had introduced us, how did he know that? He must have been briefed in the same way as the Sandbrookes. They were all in it together.

HECUBA *(realizing)* Of course. *(annoyed)* And I missed that, fool that I was.

PHILLIPA As soon as he died, I began to realize the house was what they were after, and I couldn't have that, could I? If she and the Sandbrookes wiped Vesta's side of the family out, where would that have left me? If they owned the house, there'd be no chance of a place in the vault when my time came. And that's mine by right.

HECUBA *(with curiousity)* But how did you know he *(indicating* **ANTHONY**'s *body)* was Postumus Tomb? None of the others had a clue.

PHILLIPA *(drily)* As you mentioned earlier – the Tombs have very distinctive features. So when we went into the kitchen, I told him who I was, what we needed to do, and was waiting behind the panel there when Cicely died so unexpectedly. I knew you hadn't poisoned the brandy, so it meant a quick change of plan and I only just managed to warn him before she put in her appearance.

HECUBA *(understanding)* So that's why he said you were dead?

PHILLIPA I hadn't been entirely sure the Sandbrookes were working together, but we had to give the impression that Posti had killed me, in order to find out. I warned him not to tell you in case whichever it was overheard, and struck first. *(grimacing)* Pity you finished him off before we had a chance to explain. *(heavily)* Still...he was upset about Drusilla, and was planning to kill you before we'd even settled this business. Something I talked him out of, of course. I mean...I couldn't let him kill you. And as things worked out, the most intelligent Tomb's still here. *(smiling at her)* As Papa used to say, "In this family, darling, survival's just a good example of insufficient planning".

She rises.

HECUBA *(surprised)* You're not going?

She rises anxiously.

PHILLIPA Of course not. There's the bodies to dispose of. The marsh, I think. Don't you?

HECUBA *(fussily)* Oh, Monica... You're so clever. If only we'd met before.

PHILLIPA *(smiling)* Well, at least I know the business will be in safe hands. *(kissing* HECUBA *lightly on the cheeks)* I'll get the wheelbarrow. *(moving towards the door)* There're nine bodies to move. Remember?

HECUBA *(frowning)* Nine?

PHILLIPA *(turning back)* Danesworth. Sir Beverley. Miss Venner. Drusilla. Daphne. And these three.

She indicates the bodies.

HECUBA But that's only eight.

PHILLIPA *(realizing and speaking brightly)* Oh, yes. I'd forgotten yours, hadn't I?

HECUBA *gapes at her.*

(beaming) The kiss I just gave you. There's a small additive mixed in with my lipstick. Something Dora came up with a few years ago. Acts within minutes. *(explaining)* Dizziness and nausea, followed by paralysis and heart failure. Quite ingenious, isn't it? I use a special coating to keep it off my own skin, but it'll easily penetrate your face powder. *(smiling)* She really was a genius, don't you think?

HECUBA *(horrified)* I don't believe you.

She rubs frantically at her cheek.

PHILLIPA It's no use rubbing. You're showing signs already. *(as cold as ice)* I couldn't care less about the rest of them, but you really shouldn't have poisoned Daphne – even if it was by accident. You've no idea how difficult it is, finding a good editor. My next book could be delayed by months.

HECUBA *(frantically)* But you can't write another. You're dying. You said so.

PHILLIPA *(shaking her head)* Oh, Hecuba. Didn't you learn anything from your years with Vesta? Never trust a Tomb. *(sighing)* I said my condition was incurable, and Monica Tomb would cease to exist in six weeks' time, which is absolutely true. It's just a pity you interpreted it the wrong way. There's no cure for love, and I'm marrying a sweet little man from Camden Town, changing my surname to his, and moving to somewhere a little more – picturesque, shall we say?

HECUBA *slowly subsides onto the settee.*

Sorry I can't invite you, but at least you've got what you've always wanted. After three hundred years, you'll be the last one of our particular line to bear the name of Tomb. How's that for recognition?

PHILLIPA *exits leaving the dying* **HECUBA** *sprawled on the settee.*

Curtain.

FURNITURE AND PROPERTY LIST

ACT I

Scene One

Onstage: Black walnut fireplace. *On the outer edges of the mantle:* outsize vases. *Above it:* painting with thick frame
Carved wooden fender
Huge fire-dog of brass with attendant implements
Hearthrug
Bookcases
Pelmets and coffee-colou red net curtains. *Hanging from them:* thick velvet drapes
Drinks table. *On it:* table lamp, decanters, soda syphon, tray of glasses
Winged armchair
Cabinet. *On it:* lamp, bowl of snowdrops, assorted knick-knacks
Matching cabinet. *On it:* dried flowers
Writing desk. *On it:* pens, blotter, bottle of ink. *In it:* writing papers, envelopes
Telephone
Settee
Narrow table stand

Off stage: Old- fashioned diary (**Drusilla**)

Personal: **Drusilla:** mobile phone
Hecuba: ornamental hair pins
Sir Beverley: inhaler
Robert: mobile phone
Quentin: key ring. *Attached to it:* small torch

Scene Two

Off stage: Latex gloves, a dish of Turkish Delight, a tray. *On it:* china cup and saucer, spoon, milk jug and sugar bowl (**Hecuba**)

Personal: **Phillipa:** handbag
Daphne: handbag
Quentin: rings
Cicely: handbag

ACT II

Scene One

Off stage: Tray. *On it:* cup of tea (**Hecuba**)
Gun (**Gloved hand**)

Personal: **Drusilla:** handkerchief, mobile
Cicely: handbag
Sir Beverley: inhaler

Scene Two

Off stage: Gun (**Anthony**)

LIGHTING PLOT

Property fitting required: nil
One interior set

ACT I, Scene One

To open: General interior lighting

Cue 1   **Drusilla:** "...none of them leaves here alive."
       and **Hecuba** gives a delighted smile   (Page 29)
       Blackout

ACT I, Scene Two

To open: General interior lighting

Cue 2   **Daphne** topples sideways onto the settee   (Page 50)
       Light fade

ACT II, Scene One

To open: General interior lighting

Cue 3   **Miranda:** "It's the name I was christened
       with."   (Page 74)
       Light fade

ACT II, Scene Two

To open: General interior lighting

No cues

EFFECTS PLOT

ACT I

Cue 1   **Hecuba:** "Do give me some credit, Drusilla.
       Now Vesta's gone—"   (Page 6)
       Heavy pounding at main door

Cue 2   **Drusilla:** "Between the other two, they'd
       wiped out most of the family."   (Page 7)
       Knocking comes again

Cue 3   **Hecuba** glances round the room then
       exits   (Page 33)
       Tapping sound

Cue 4   **Hecuba:** "But I particularly made this
       for you."   (Page 46)
       Internal telephone rings

ACT II

Cue 5   **Drusilla:** "What are you doing? I told you
       not to—"   (Page 72)
       Gun fires

Cue 6   **Miranda:** "I can manage the rest on my
       own, now." She points the gun at
       Robert and pulls the trigger   (Page 92)
       Gun fires

FIREARMS AND OTHER WEAPONS USED IN THEATRE PRODUCTIONS

With regards to the rules and regulations of firearms and other weapons used in theatre productions, we recommend that you read the Entertainment Information Sheet No. 20 (Health and Safety Executive).

This information sheet is one of a series produced in consultation with the Joint Advisory Committee for Broadcasting and the Performing Arts. It gives guidance on the management of weapons that are part of a production, including firearms, replicas and deactivated weapons.

This sheet may be downloaded from: www.hse.gov.uk. Alternatively, you can contact HSE Books, P O Box 1999, Sudbury, Suffolk, CO10 2WA Tel: 01787 881165 Fax: 01787 313995.